So This Is Where We Stand?

So This Is Where We Stand?

**How Western Thinking Has Changed
over the Last Five Hundred Years**

Giovanni Burrascano

 iUniverse®

SO THIS IS WHERE WE STAND?
HOW WESTERN THINKING HAS CHANGED OVER THE LAST FIVE HUNDRED YEARS

iUniverse books may be ordered through booksellers or by contacting:

iUniverse
1663 Liberty Drive
Bloomington, IN 47403
www.iuniverse.com
1-800-Authors (1-800-288-4677)

ISBN: 978-1-5320-0229-8 (sc)
ISBN: 978-1-5320-0230-4 (e)

Library of Congress Control Number: 2016911428

Print information available on the last page.

iUniverse rev. date: 09/12/2016

Contents

Part I
The "Advanced" World

Part II
The Underdeveloped World within Us: The Case of Latin America

Part III
The Circumpolar North

Part IV
Some Observations

To my amazing mother and father

Preface

I vividly remember one early-summer night in LaSalle, Québec, when I was fourteen or fifteen. I sat on the front steps of my parent's house. To my left, my father leaned with his arms crossed over the balcony fence, taking in the beautiful weather the day had offered. It was a perfect night, no wind, with little humidity, and it was so clear I could see shining stars everywhere in the sky. In a quick instant, I turned and suddenly asked, "Dad, why is the world the way it is?" With all his heart, he tried to give me an explanation, and I was happy with that. After all, I'd caught him off guard with that question and felt bad for him. For years, I never raised this question again.

I also remember visiting a library during my youth and telling myself that someday I would like to write a book and see it displayed on a library shelf along with all the others. As I grew older, my interests were with school, friends, sports, girls, and eventually preuniversity studies, cars, dating, music and being a disc jockey, going out with friends, travel, work, and community involvement. In my mid to late twenties, around 1988–1991, I was quite active in the local community in which I grew up, performing volunteer work of different sorts, including a public seminar I gave on the topic of the greenhouse effect and inadvertent global climatic change. I was probably one of the few, if not the first, to discuss this topic in the public arena of my community at that time, when this issue was not widely known. I was virtually ridiculed by some for doing so. Life kept me busy, and I guess I kept exploring and learning. I certainly wasn't thinking about writing a book during those periods of my life.

Eventually, marriage at the age of twenty-nine in 1992 kept me busy on many fronts. However, it had a calming and nurturing effect on me, and in 1994 I was inspired enough to put pen to paper and write. This work you're about to read has been in the making for a long time and is the culmination of a lifelong dream. I pondered on an array of subjects about which to write. Many areas of life were interesting to me. However, for some reason, for the longest time I had been interested in the European medieval period, the Industrial Revolution, and the associated urbanization. Some people who know me well enough have actually called me the Renaissance man. In university, between 1983 and 1986, some student colleagues would refer to me as "the scanner" because they saw in me the ability to easily scan and size up concepts, notions, trends, and situations and convey them in a concise, clear manner. I am a generalist and like a more all-encompassing explanation of things; this provides the foundation for the topic at hand.

Between 1980 and 1982, I studied at the pre-university level and earned a diploma in social sciences from Dawson College, Montreal, Canada. A lot of the curriculum involved courses in geography and psychology. In 1986, I received a bachelor's degree in geography, specializing in a program called urban systems, from McGill University in Montreal, which included a strong dose of courses in environmental studies and political science. In 1989, I also completed management studies at Concordia University, Montreal. I have had an extensive career in commercial real estate and construction in Montreal. In the last nineteen years (1997–2016), fourteen years have been centered on regional economic development at the paramunicipal level of government, and I spent five years as vice president of business development for an important Montreal commercial builder. Employed in the realm of regional economic development, I view myself as being part of the solution to worldly problems.

In relation to this treatise, having an academic background in geography, a social and physical science, allows me to apply knowledge and approaches from this field of study in comprehending why, how, and when the physical world affects humans, and how humans affect the physical world. Geography is the only academic discipline that seeks understanding of the interaction between humans and the physical world, ultimately providing a more complete picture of phenomena; it uses a multidisciplinary approach to understanding. Treated in this analysis is why and how Western thought has changed and spread worldwide over the last five hundred years, and its effects on nature and you.

The reason for writing this piece is sevenfold. First, I felt the desire to understand more and place my compartmentalized knowledge and life experience in proper perspective with the world. Intertwined (perhaps subconsciously) with that, I sought to obtain a more profound and complete answer that on that special night my very honorable and loving dad, and many persons and written sources thereafter, could not provide with more breadth. Second, I had the realization at some point that since graduating from university in 1986, nothing has really changed in the world. The third world still existed, many of the social and environmental ills of our time still persist and became exacerbated, and new such problems came to surface years after the completion of my education. Third, I have a sincere concern for social and environmental issues, and I would like to see overall improvement on a worldwide scale. Fourth, I desired to crystallize the pattern involved with how Western political-economic expansion unfolds and impacts the wider world's societies and nature. Fifth, I wanted to highlight that new economic and cultural trends are on the rise, and norms are in formation and on their way to changing Western culture and society. Sixth, I could call out to the leaders of Western education systems and invite them to consider that curriculums must include more required study of history and social and environmental science, particularly in fields that are very specialized. This would create students with a more complete understanding of where their fields of study belong in the world and how they can contribute. Finally, I enjoy writing, and in the words of American philosopher, self-help author, and motivational speaker Wayne Dyer, "Don't die with your music still in you." In the same vein, a few years ago I visited an exposition of ancient artifacts at a local museum. On one of the walls was written something to the effect of "People leave this world, but the art remains."

This treatise unites historical and contemporary facts to the point where one can grasp a clearer picture of where we and the world stand. It provides answers to many questions. It helps complete one's understanding of the world by viewing things from a more macro perspective, rather than a micro one. Our academic disciplines are by and large graduating very intelligent persons in specialized fields, often at the expense of a better understanding of how, historically, humanity has reached today.

Life is a long journey, and many have not had the opportunity or the time to sit back and ponder on the status of the world, or even their own lives. Many people have questions. This is why this work is unique: it provides, in one volume, a well-rounded treatment of why we think the way we do and from where today's social and environmental ills stem. Understanding history makes one understand society today and one's place in the world, and it helps our wider society better define the path it can take. For you, it can fill voids. If you do not already have some grasp of what's covered herein, you're missing the big picture about living in this day and age.

I am concerned about our many social and environmental problems. The intention of this work is to provide readers from all walks of life with information about social and environmental issues that surround them every day, with the hope that understanding can lead to solutions and prevent the development of other problems. The challenges we face today are not solely the responsibility of our governments, but also of every human living on our planet.

I have lived my life in the capitalist Western world and have enjoyed what life has to offer. However, a part of me hurts deep inside. I hurt because of what I have witnessed being done to people and what our species is in the process of doing to the very organism that sustains all life—our planet.

The natural world is threatened by human activity, no matter how much we may try to hide that fact or distract attention from it. This means that the survival of the human species is also threatened. The manner in which we choose to live is self-defeating on multiple fronts, as are many of the ways we choose to treat one another.

I do not want you to think that I live as a pessimist; in no way would that be representative of me. I live a happy and (depending on how one defines it) privileged life. I feel the need to express what so many are afraid to express, don't understand, or can't be bothered with.

In my opinion, this work is beneficial for the mind. It helps us understand the interconnected forces at work that affect us every day. Understanding what is taking place calms my mind, because I then do not need to wonder any longer about what has caused the problems I see surrounding us. After achieving such an understanding, the only thing left is to do something about them! I have tried to accomplish this in many ways, and this work is yet another way.

I spent a considerable amount of time completing this document, and I enjoyed every minute because the subject at hand is an important one. I find this work to provide a perspective that reminds us of how fragile we really are and how precarious our very existence is on this stunningly beautiful globe we call home. Understanding this, one sees firsthand how magical life is, and how wonderful it can be when we eliminate from our minds much of the superficiality and nonsense surrounding us.

Introduction

On Christmas Eve, 1986, at Granddad Tom's house, located in suburban Chicago, the whole family was gathered to celebrate this wondrous occasion amid joyful relatives, lots of food, beautiful Christmas decor, a Christmas tree displaying gifts for all standing tall in the corner next to the warm fireplace, and near blizzard conditions outside. At the party were cousins Anthony and Sam, who happened to be sitting next to each other on the living room sofa in front of the fireplace, discussing the usual topics that arise anytime the family was together— topics such as religion, politics, economics, and business. While conversing over some chilled white wine, Anthony suddenly interjected and asked Sam, "Did you watch the documentary on TV last week?"

Sam replied, "No, what was it all about?"

Anthony happily explained that it was a show in which the world was the stage, the biosphere the setting, and seven billion humans were the actors. Anthony hesitated and then continued his description. What Anthony tried to convey to his cousin was profound because it focused on human activity on earth. The human activity that has taken place over the last four hundred years in particular is worrisome. The evolution of Western thinking has created many marvelous human aspirations, such as sending humans to the moon, man-made artistic beauty and functionality in landscape architecture, the fine arts, architecture, civil engineering of all sorts, chemistry, medicine and biotechnology, food production and preservation, transportation, construction, mechanics, electronics, and communications. However, it is also true that these same marvels stemming from human thinking have inflicted great pain on Mother Earth, the very organism that sustains all life.

The following account is a general treatment of human thinking over the last five hundred years, which has shaped the human condition and its human relationship with earth. The focus is on Western civilization's thinking and how it has been diffused from the Western world to global proportions, affecting almost all cultures. Citizens of the Western world believe that their way of thinking is the correct or only way of thinking, and in purposeful or often inadvertent ways they influence all other cultures and impact the earth. One of the perspectives used here is that of the geographer in order to analyze the effects of the last five hundred years of human thinking on Mother Earth, because it appears to provide an increasingly important approach to understanding how humanity uses the space on earth to carry forth its objectives, whatever they may be.

An attempt has been made to present this analysis in a multidisciplinary, holistic manner in order to demonstrate the effectiveness of a generalistic approach, and to illustrate the direction humanity has taken in its relationship to earth. This approach may not encompass every combination and permutation of contemporary or world history or of factual information, and it is not intended to because in the final analysis, the attempt made is one that offers a glimpse of our world in her present standing.

Not only is earth being used in harmful ways by humanity, but earth is responding to humanity in health-threatening ways and will increasingly force us to listen to what she is saying for human survival is threatened. At the heart of it all, Mother Earth's message to humankind is that it is time to change certain key elements found in our way of thinking and adopt values and beliefs that are in accordance with environmental systems and their limitations. By extension, the manner in which humans treat other humans must also be reevaluated.

This analysis is divided into four parts. The first deals with the advanced world. An introduction to general systems theory is provided and discusses the influence of the Judeo-Christian religion and science in the shaping of Western thought. A discussion on the scientific revolution, colonialism, imperialism, and capitalism ensues, followed by descriptions of Western industrialization and urbanization and their associated environmental impacts. Subsequent parts attempt to demonstrate the spatial diffusion of Western thinking to global proportions, with particular attention given to the less developed world and the circumpolar north. The second part therefore focuses on the underdeveloped world with special reference to the Latin American experience. Here, colonialism and dependency are discussed, as well as new dependency, the role of urbanization in Western economic expansion, and social and environmental impacts. The third part deals with the circumpolar north, which demonstrates the more recent modern expansion of Western thinking into polar regions. The focus is on the stages of economic development of the north and their social, political, economic, and environmental impacts. The final section of this work offers some personal observations, and conclusions are provided.

Part I

The "Advanced" World

Chapter 1

A Framework to Understanding

General Systems Theory

The following discussion of general systems theory is provided because it lays a good foundation for understanding contemporary economic, social, cultural, political, and environmental issues. This type of approach encourages a multidisciplinary perspective on issues, which can bring to light a more complete understanding of, and hopefully solutions to, given problems and issues. The systemic approach is not necessarily the only one that can be employed, but it can be useful in seeking understanding and solutions when combined with other models and approaches.

Davidson (1983) says that Austrian biologist and philosopher Ludwig Von Bertalanffy is considered the father of general systems theory. Bertalanffy believed that modern society requires a new way of thinking. He believed that a holistic perspective on problems and issues is required in modern society. The words *synthesis, integrative, organismic, ecological, synergistic,* and *systemic* can be used to describe holistic thinking.

Based on his biological research, Bertalanffy presented the important concept of the living organism as an organized system. A living organism survives because its parts and processes are organized for the survival of the whole entity. Just as important is Bertalanffy's concept of the living organism as an open system. This means that an entity is not only interacting within itself but also with its external environment. These concepts have great revolutionary implications for modern society because they could be applied not only to biology as a science but also to other realms such as social institutions and behavioral and social science.

The Bertalanffian systemic approach theory was a proposed scientific discipline that was intended to unite science. It is a scientific breakthrough because knowledge about all systems could be used by humanity in order to enhance the abilities of prediction and control in physical, biological, behavioral, and sociological aspects of our society. Although many scientists from many different fields have tried to apply it, this scientific discipline is still an aspiration. However, it is seen today as an approach, attitude, or viewpoint in understanding and resolving problems and issues, rather than a discipline in itself.

Bertalanffy's general systems theory is much broader in scope than the systemic approaches often applied by engineers. It is a much more all-encompassing, multidisciplinary way to approach problems and issues. For instance, a Bertalanffian system can be described in various ways: (a) physical like a computer, biological like a cat, psychological like a personality, sociological like a community volunteer club, or symbolic like laws; (b) as a combination such as humans working with machines in a factory, static like a rock, mechanical like a watch, mechanically self-regulating like a thermostat, or organismically interactive with the environment such as plants and people; (c) as being composed of smaller and bigger systems, such as a province or state having smaller municipal jurisdictions and also being part of a country, a system or subsystem, or hierarchical.

In defining the word *system,* the word *interaction* plays a vital role because it leads to the meaning of entities not standing alone but in interaction with its organized relationship of parts and external environment. For example, without the organized interaction of parts in a wristwatch, it could not function within its casing. Further, an entity interacts with itself and the external environment such as people do in cities or bees do in a beehive.

Bertalanffy urged that society learn to "think interaction" in all aspects of our lives; he advocated that we dare to broaden our perspective from nation to globe. This certainly sheds light on the important fact that if we want to find solutions to modern day problems, we must first understand in detail the whole system.

The major reason for integrating a brief discussion of Bertalanffy's theory in this analysis is because modern Western society is only now beginning to open its mind to having a fresher, wider perspective on issues. In large part, Western culture is still heavily dependent on a more compartmentalized approach to problems and issues, and to life in general. This means that Western society relies too much on specifics rather than having a wider perspective as suggested by the Bertalanffian theory. The results of thinking specific are evident: Western civilization has benefited in many regards, such as the invention of sophisticated technologies for all kinds of purposes, medical breakthroughs in drug treatments, and high-tech machines used in other industries. This way of thinking has not necessarily been totally beneficial because many modern problems are still left unresolved or have been exacerbated even further.

Chapter 2

The Influence of Science

The Scientific Revolution

Today's Western values and the manner in which Westerners now view the world are rooted in the sixteenth and seventeenth centuries. It was between 1500 and 1700 that there was an important shift in the way people saw the world and in their way of thinking. Before the year 1500, the leading world view in Europe and in most other civilizations was more natural and spiritual. This meant that people lived in small communities, they shared with their neighbors, and individual needs were seen as less important than those of the wider community.

Medieval science was based on logic and religious belief in order to understand life at that point in time. God, the stars, the human spirit, and ethics provided the foundation for explanation of life and phenomena. Thinking changed with time, and gradually new scientific methodology and ideas were used to explain life and phenomena. This was the beginning of a new science that took on a new feel and importance. As this "new science" evolved, so did people's perception of the world and what they valued and believed. With the evolution of science came an evolution in the way people perceived the world and the values and beliefs they adhered to, including the way they viewed the natural environment.

Why discuss the scientific revolution? It is important to understand this period of our Western civilization because its consequences have been so far-reaching. The scientific revolution influenced our lives and wider society in multitudinous ways. As the scientific revolution evolved, it brought with it more and increasingly rapid changes in the ways people live and approach life, as exemplified in the invention of the automobile and the arrival of advanced computer technology. The key thing to remember is that the manner in which we live today, the way we perceive things to be, and what we envision for the future are based on changes that have occurred in the course of history, particularly over the last five hundred years. The earth has existed for four billion years, and many civilizations and revolutions shaped the periods leading up to the year 1500. The last five hundred years are when the greatest and most rapid changes in thought have occurred, which makes this period of world history most significant because we are now witnessing what we currently believe can be detrimental to the earth as a physical entity, as well as to its life forms—including our species.

Are competition and survival of the fittest the way life should be? Is the kind of progress we have experienced truly progress? Where do our conceptions of life come from? You will discover that notions developed by humans have largely shaped today's reality. The problem is that many of those notions have been founded on inadequate knowledge in many fields. Today, we still walk a path that was paved hundreds of years ago by those who were working with information and materials inferior to those available today. Thus, we are now caught in a manner of living that is based on old conceptions of life and how it should be led. We humans have acknowledged that Western thought from the past five centuries has put the world on a course that threatens survival on this planet. Humanity needs to change important aspects involved with surviving on earth. Yes, we are doing it to ourselves! Globalization of current Western thought will eventually be viewed as another revolution in itself because the rest of the world will become caught up in the same vortex the Western world is caught up in now. To understand where we are heading, we must look back at the significant changes in thought that were brought about by science and the role of religion.

Even with all the factual knowledge we now have in our possession, is globalization creating a new path for humanity to take us in a better direction, or is it just one more step on the old path set in front of us by those who understood less in the past?

A portion of the remainder of this chapter is based on the work of Austrian-born American physicist, educator, and author of several important books, Fritjof Capra, from his masterpiece *The Turning Point* (1983). Capra describes how the scientific revolution occurred between the sixteenth and seventeenth centuries, commencing with Nicolas Copernicus and Johannes Kepler, who both diminished the role of divine intervention as the explanation of life and phenomena and put emphasis on mathematics as the explanation. An even greater emphasis was put on mathematics as the explanation of life and phenomena by Galileo Galilei, considered the creator of modern science. He is responsible for the explanation of the laws of falling masses and was the first in history to utilize scientific experimentation and mathematics together to explain these laws and nature. This new approach in science and to understanding became extremely important in the seventeenth century, and it is still the manner in which scientists approach questions regarding nature, life, and the universe. As a result, the world of science, with massive reliance on empiricism as the explanation of life and nature, no longer entered more humanly and spiritual factors in the equation of understanding life and nature. Thus, the five senses, religion, feelings, values and beliefs, and the human spirit became insignificant in this new science. At no time is this new scientific approach more evident than in the seventeenth century, when Englishman Francis Bacon postulated that nature was to be subdued by humanity and serve the best interests of humankind in order to relieve hardship and inconvenience. This notion took on great importance in wider society because it was given support by the Church, an establishment that prior to Bacon was against any other description of the natural world and the universe. The Church agreed with Bacon because he presented the enslavement of nature by humans via science as God's will and glory, as well as a human right. This approach to life has essentially been the way in which humanity has privileged itself over the fish of the sea and the earth's flora, fauna, and underground resources. Has this joining of science and religion been heavily misconstrued by Westerners, whereby those who stood to benefit from power and wealth could subdue and rape the earth and cause the subordination of other countries and their peoples via colonialism during the rise of industrialism and capitalism?

Thus humans, in the image of God and at the hierarchical pinnacle in the chain of being (also known as the Ladder of Creation), had the right to treat any other species and the entire planet as it pleased because humankind was considered more important. This is a form of chauvinism. In a paper that I self-published focusing on the Great Chain of Being (2002: 13–15, 17–18), I state that in order to understand when human chauvinism began to rise significantly and to comprehend the role of religion in the expansion of Western power and capitalism, we must look further into history. One factor inherent in the Christian religion is called the Great

Chain of Being, an ancient Greek belief that dates before Aristotle and that said that all living things are categorized by rank and in hierarchical fashion. This idea tried to explain the grand conception of the plan and structure of the world, and through the Middle Ages and up to the late eighteenth century, most educated persons accepted it without question. The idea of the Chain of Being was first systematized by the Neoplatonist Plotinus, though the component concepts were derived from Plato and Aristotle. During the eighteenth century, aside from the word *nature*, the Great Chain of Being was a very important phrase. There existed no other period in which "writers of all sorts—men of science and philosophers, poets and popular essayists, deists and orthodox divines—talked so much about the Chain of Being, or accepted more implicitly the general scheme of ideas connected with it, or more boldly drew from these their latent implications, or apparent implications" (Lovejoy, 1936: 183). Christian scholars assumed that all aspects of the world could be ranked in a hierarchy of worth. At the top of the hierarchy is a being in the likeness of God, humankind, with all his perfection in mind and body. All other forms of life in the hierarchy are placed below humankind and are considered less advanced, and each is less advanced than the next down the hierarchy, until rock and metal material is reached, and finally hell. Within each of these large groups there were subhierarchies. For example, among rock and metal materials, gold was the noblest and stood highest. There was a similar ranking with vegetation and animals, and even humans, because it was also implied that there existed a ranking of humankind itself in which Europeans were at the top of the hierarchy, followed by Asians and Americans, and Africans; whites were positioned above blacks, and males over females. The wealthy were positioned above the poor. It was accepted that such a hierarchical order of being always existed, was universal rule, and was eternal.

Particularly because humankind in the image of God had more spirit, and thus was placed at the hierarchical pinnacle in the Chain of Being, it had the right to treat any other species and nature as it pleased because humans were considered more important than anything else. This is a glorification of human beings, and as such, it's human chauvinism. Victorian England can be used as an illustration of a society that believed society improved in a progressive manner, that the catalyst for progress was struggle and competition, and that this was the will of God. This society was conditioned to viewing life as hierarchical, as being in rank and progressive, and it was believed that only the best survived. Those who survived and were considered successful in life based on aggressiveness, material, and power were deemed better (winners) than those who were deemed not successful (losers) in competitive society. Thus, they projected this same line of thinking upon comparisons made of themselves to other nations, concluding that industrial England and Europe were superior to other global cultures and societies. Our perspective of the world, including a scientific opinion about nature, is a product of the society in which we live.

The English naturalist and geologist recognized for his contributions to evolutionary theory, Charles Darwin, presented in his book *On the Origin of Species* (1859) a theory of evolution to explain biological change. His theory is considered brilliant by many, but it is limited by the era in which he lived, nineteenth-century establishment England. Darwin believed that God created the world, and he was well read on social, economic, and political literature of the time. In nineteenth-century England, the social belief system was that society improved in a progressive manner, and that the catalyst for progress was struggle and competition both domestically and internationally; this was the will of God. When Darwin arrived in the Galapagos Islands, he brought with him the cultural conditioning he had been exposed to, and thus he was already predisposed to viewing nature as hierarchical, as being in rank and progressive. He inevitably projected this thinking on nature by concluding that only through natural selection did improvement of species take place, meaning that only the best survived and those that survived were more advanced than predecessors. This "survival of the fittest" concept is descriptive of the struggles involved with economically harsh Victorian and capitalist societies.

It appears that from the Western cultural acceptance of the fact that humans are more important than anything else, many Western traits emanate from this linear reasoning, and there was and still is gravitation toward its philosophy in the many activities of humanity to the present day. Leaders of the scientific revolution such as Galileo, Newton, Descartes, Locke, and Hobbes brought about the eventual collapse of the hierarchical outlook on life, but there are many extremely powerful attributes from past hierarchical thinking that we still use every day, and most people are not aware of where their thinking stems from or why they apply it.

I also state in my self-published paper that power, coercion, and hierarchical relations insinuate the same thing. Power is not a thing and is not a property of any individual, but it appears as an ability to overtake or control others and things. French sociologist, anthropologist, and ethnologist Georges Balandier states "power is strengthened by the accentuation of inequalities ... [such as the use of bureaucracy]" (1972: 37–45). This is what is happening in the modern world. It is the underlying reason why three-quarters of the world population still lives in poor conditions, and why nature is subdued by humans. Power exists in primitive societies, but it manifests itself differently than in our culture. For instance, in our culture there exists political power, which is based upon economic strength and (at extremes) military might. It is not comparable to almost any other global society. In comparison, on a more micro scale, in primitive societies, power, status, and prestige are based on softer distance to ancestors, kinship ties, age, and gender. In our society power, status, and prestige are based on competitiveness, hierarchy, social class, and wealth. It's now based on individual demeanor, the type of car one owns, the type of employment one has, or the size of living accommodations one is able to afford.

Any manner one wants to view at all of this, the Western world has the power to impose itself on all other societies and introduces a lifestyle that causes acculturation and absorbs them into the Western sphere of influence and control. Northern native communities and less developed nations are examples of this.

During the seventeenth century, aside from Newton, a figure that greatly contributed to change in scientific and Western thought was Descartes. He sought "the scientific truth." This is a science that sought perfection in the explanation of life and the universe. There was no place for chance or probability, only certainty from empiricism. It is well-known today that there is no complete explanation of matters in science and that it offers only approximations of life and natural phenomena. Much of Western society still follows this belief that science is the only explanation in comprehending the world and universe. According to Descartes, nature and the universe worked like a machine using intricate mechanical laws and the arrangement and movement of its parts. In relation to this line of thinking, people's perception of nature changed because they no longer viewed nature as organic but as machinelike, and it led humans to treat nature with less respect, leading to the mass exploitation we witness today. Descartes's scientific approach is analytical because it is based on breaking up thoughts and problems into parts and reorganizing them into a logical order. This approach is considered to be a great contribution to science because it has led to the development of scientific theories and complex technological advancements. However, this type of thinking has caused us to view life and phenomena in a divisive and compartmentalized manner, and not in an integrated, holistic way. This is why we view the mind as superior to the body, or we believe that mental work is superior to manual work, or why it is difficult to remedy diseases that exist because we focus too much on the disease and not the wider social or environmental circumstances surrounding them.

The scientific revolution was completed by Isaac Newton, born in England in 1642. Newton developed a complete mathematical formulation of the mechanist view of nature and thus created a work that unified the previous works of Copernicus, Kepler, Galileo, Bacon, and Descartes. In the seventeenth century, Newton was considered the Einstein of today. His understanding of mathematics was more advanced than any of the individuals who attempted to explain nature before him. For Newton, the universe was still one huge, mechanical system operating according to precise mathematical laws. With his invention of differential calculus, he formulated the exact laws of motion for all bodies under the influence of the force of gravity. Newton's explanation of these laws was significant during his time because they were found to be valid throughout the solar system, and this confirmed once again the mechanical view of nature. God was no longer used as an explanation for nature; for Newton, God was the creator of the material particles, the forces between them, and the laws of motion. Thus God was implied, however the physical phenomena themselves were not considered to be divine at all. When it became increasingly possible to describe nature mathematically, belief in the divine disappeared completely from science. This explains why there exists much less spirituality in our present culture. The objective description of nature without human interference of any kind became the ideal of all science, which is still true today. The success of Newtonian physics and Descartes's belief in the certainty of scientific knowledge led to a strong emphasis on physical science and hard technology. This was part of the eighteenth-century Age of Enlightenment and still influences us today.

It is vital to underline that during the scientific revolution, two distinct correlations were taking place. These correlations are omnipresent in today's culture. They were largely evident during the period of Newtonian science. First, as science began to rely increasingly upon mathematics to explain nature and the universe, the explanatory value of God as an active factor in the operation of nature and the physical world decreased in importance. As religious influences decreased in science, they also decreased in the wider society. In today's Western culture, we are witnessing a decline in the importance of religion both as an institution and in the lives of individuals. The second evident correlation is that as belief in the notion of scientific truth strengthened, so did the scientific community's emphasis on the physical sciences and hard technology. This explains why our modern Western culture is so reliant upon and entrenched in technology of all sorts.

During the nineteenth century scientists still used the mechanistic view of the world in physics, chemistry, biology, psychology, and social sciences. During the same period, however, new discoveries such as electric and magnetic phenomena were made that could not be explained by Newtonian mechanist approaches, and they laid the groundwork that would transcend Newtonian thinking and open science to the twentieth century. The theory of evolution was born in geology during the nineteenth century and further eroded Newtonian thinking; this forced scientists to abandon the view of the world as a machine created by God and adopt the notion that the universe was in fact an evolutionary and altering system in which simple forms of life developed into intricately more sophisticated ones. Capra (1983: 74) states:

At the end of the nineteenth century Newtonian mechanics had lost its role as the fundamental theory of natural phenomena. Maxwell's electrodynamics and Darwin's theory of evolution involved concepts that were significantly far more advanced than the Newtonian model and indicated that the universe was far more complex than Descartes and Newton had imagined.

Einstein's theory of relativity and quantum physics convincingly proved this as well. Nature and the universe are no longer perceived as a machine, but rather as an interconnected web of patterns and processes, as proposed by Bertalanffy.

It is evident that science has had a major impact on Western culture and thinking over the last five hundred years. As science adopted different views of the world, from Copernicus to Einstein, correlated changes in Western conditions, values, and beliefs occurred. The influence of religion in explaining the universe is now nonexistent in science because only the scientific truth is sought. However, religion has played and continues to play a role in the way Western society thinks. Further elaboration on this matter will be provided in an upcoming section of this analysis.

Although the present scientific community is increasingly adopting a more organic view of the universe, Western society has still not significantly distanced itself from scientific influences of thought from the past. Our politics, economics, culture, society, and environment are presently caught in a vortex of cause and effect and a standard of living that is based upon and dependent upon the older ways of thinking. The best example of this is the concept of economic growth, where today's politicians, economists, and business elite depend upon and wish for more economic growth, profits, and job creation. Our society's addiction to the economic growth factor in the industrial economies of the world is highly correlated with technological growth. Individuals and corporate institutions are amazed by modern technology and have come to think that almost all problems in modern society can be solved with technical solutions. No matter the type of problem involved, if it is political, environmental, or medical, our society's automatic response is to apply existing technology or develop a new technology to fix the problem. Examples of this are the use of sophisticated missiles and bombs in modern warfare to solve a problem between nations, or the development and use of chemicals to grow higher quantities of food.

Western thinking has been diffused throughout the world by different means and for different reasons. Excluding a prolonged discussion on human curiosity and discovery and the historical importance of technology, such as sail ships (which allowed for the exploration of unknown lands, such as in the case of Columbus's discovery of the Americas in 1492) and the resultant influential intervention of Western thought in often indigenous societies, we now explore more contemporary reasons regarding why and how the world is becoming Westernized and the implications of this rising trend.

Chapter 3

The Westernization of the Globe

Colonialism, Imperialism, Capitalism

The Industrial Revolution of 1820–1913 characterizes our modern economic growth because it is during this era that science was applied to technology. Technological progress made during this period was the cause of unprecedented levels of economic changes and growth, recording incredible increases in GNP and personal income in countries of the Organization for Economic Co-operation and Development, otherwise known as the OECD. This level of growth was unimaginable during the 1700s. The era witnessed a huge decrease in the employment of people in agriculture, bringing the level of urbanization to new heights. This setting allowed for more effective information exchange, further compounding scientific and technological advancements; a massive rise in the volume of unrestricted and low or free tariff and barrier world export (which happened because of the invention of the steamship and later the refrigerated steamship); the beginnings of a global economy and more integrated global financial system; the international movement of capital and people; the amplification of social stratification; and the creation of richer and poorer nations.

There existed a different world order and world economy prior to 1500. Economic activities of different types took place between geographic areas like Asia and Africa, particularly trade. Europe eventually became a fertile ground for intensified colonialism because of a variety of shaping events taking place within its political boundaries and outside its boundaries, and it would favor chief states of this continent's importance as a colonial power. More particularly, it would eventually thrust England into the so-called highest stage of capitalism. England became a major colonial power because of internal shaping events and policies and events external to England.

According to John A. Hobson, a British economist and prolific writer, the years 1884–1900 were the years of intensification of colonial expansion for chief European states. During these years, Hobson estimates that Great Britain, France, Germany, Belgium, and Portugal acquired millions of square miles of territories outside Europe. According to V. I. Lenin, the Communist leader of the Russian Revolution, "The more capitalism is developed, the more the need for raw materials is felt, the more the competition becomes, and the more feverishly the hunt for raw materials proceeds throughout the world, the more desperate becomes the struggle for the acquisition of colonies." Leonard Woolf, popular author, editor, and publisher and husband of Virginia Woolf, writes that the respective colonies acquired were often by conquest, and they were incorporated usually against the wishes of their peoples now under the autocratic rule of the European state (Wright, 1976: 62). The primary motive for acquisition of these new territories was purely economic; after all, the colonies provided the mother states with raw materials, markets, and customers. European state internal policies and structures were changed to support the capitalist motive in order to respond to the needs of capital accumulation.

For example, state resources were redirected toward the creation of transport and communication infrastructures. These changes taking place were most evident in Great Britain as it propelled itself from mercantilism to capitalism in the second half of the eighteenth century. Initiated by capitalist investment, strategic inventions brought forth the production of materials by machine. According to distinguished professor of anthropology and writer Eric Wolf (1982: 267), "The major vehicle for the transition to the capitalist mode of production was the textile industry of eighteenth century England." Later, it was the construction of railroads. Other European states and America soon followed England's example. In England, the textile trade ran into competition with Dutch and Indian competition. India in particular produced cheaper and technically better quality textiles than Europeans could. This competition forced Great Britain to intensify the use of machines in order to defeat its major competitors. Not only did the English increasingly rely on machines, but inventors soon produced textile machinery (such as weaving and spinning machines) that could provide both quantity and quality in textile products. Soon, textile production would be taken from workers who worked from homes in satellite towns, concentrating production in the new workplace, the urban factory. This new form of organizing work brought more efficiency so that the cost of machinery could pay for itself, but it changed work for the workers as well. The textile industry created the entrepreneur who owned the means of production, engineers who created textile machines, supervisors, and the working class.

Generally, men, women, and children were not initially happy with working in early British factories. However, the working class soon adapted to its new way of working when, in the mid-1800s, factory work was remunerated with differentiation in status and rewards depending on position. Factory discipline was then strengthened, and a work ethic was adopted (note that men were paid more than women at this time). By 1840, English textiles were exported to Latin America and eventually to Asia, India, and China. In terms of supply, unlike wool, England needed to import cotton. In 1787, half of its cotton came from the West Indies. By 1807, however, more than 60 percent of cotton imports came from the

United States and from the eastern Mediterranean. The cotton crop of the southeast United States, in turn, became "the most important proximate cause of expansion" in the US economy after 1815 (North, 1961: 68). At that time, cotton growing with slave labor in the United States was a profitable business, however cotton growing was not the cause of slavery. Cotton growing was an important factor in the continuance of slavery well into the nineteenth century (Wolf, 1982: 280).

Between 1826 and 1848, there was a period of contraction in the British textile industry, which created significant upheavals. To spark the economy once again, money was poured into the development of a new industry. The industry involved was railroad building. Railroads required both steel production and coal mining. This can be considered as the second phase of the Industrial Revolution because the British economy shifted reliance from cotton textiles to reliance on iron and steel. Railroad building took off as well in the United States. The industrialization of England had forward and backward linkages within Europe and abroad, and it sparked industrialization within its sphere of influence and reorganized local and international economies into sectors of supply and demand in order to feed a growing Western industrialization process. This has now caused a division in Western industrialization. First, there exist countries with an old capitalist development, such as France and Great Britain, which are now progressing slowly; and second, young capitalist powers such as the United States, Germany, and Japan have vibrant industrial expansion and growth, with America showing signs of an aging industrial infrastructure.

According to Geoffrey Barraclough, a professor of modern history at Oxford, industrialism and imperialism were revolutionary forces (Wright, 1976: 159–170). The world in 1870 and the world in 1900 were significantly different. In England, where the Industrial Revolution began early and steadily progressed, the nature of the changes after 1870 is less apparent than in other countries. On a worldwide scale, and even in continental Europe (with the sole exception of Belgium), industrialization was a product of the last quarter rather than of the first two-thirds of the nineteenth century; it was a consequence of the railway age, which had provided Europe with a new system of communication by 1870. The United States became an Atlantic country and a continental nation because of the railway. Barraclough states that the second phase of the Industrial Revolution, that of the railway age of coal and iron, was different from the first phase of textile industrialization because it was far more scientific. The second phase was less reliant on practical inventions and quicker in its impact, and it affected people's lives more than ever before.

After 1870, a third phase of industrialization took place: steel, electricity, oil, and chemicals. This phase was where the impact of science and technological advance on society was at its greatest. The internal combustion engine, the microphone, the telephone, the electric lamp, mechanized public transport, the bicycle, newsprint, the typewriter, the first synthetic fibers, and plastics made their appearance in this period. By 1903 there was the initial development of the airplane:

> Here, as elsewhere, there was necessarily a time-lag before the problems of large-scale production were solved, and some of the things we have come to regard on as normal-radio and television among them-obviously belong to a later phase. Nevertheless, it can fairly be said that, the purely practical level of daily life, a person living today who was suddenly put back into the world of 1900 would find himself on familiar ground, whereas if he returned to 1870, even in industrial Britain, the differences would probably be more striking than the similarities. In short, it was around 1900 that industrialisation began to exert its influence on living conditions of the masses in the West ... the practical inventions listed above were the consequence of a steady piecemeal development or improvement of existing processes, the overwhelming majority resulted from new materials, new sources of power, and above all else from the application of scientific knowledge to industry.
>
> Barraclough, in Wright, 1976: 161

The scientific, technological, and industrial changes created the urban and industrial society known in the Western world today. A similar process subsequently expanded into the industrially undeveloped world, which will be the topic of part 2 of this analysis. With regard to the Western world, its cities were expanding at a never-before-seen rate because of the requirements of industrialization: workers were increasingly being concentrated in factories located in existing industrial towns and urban areas. Large towns overtook satellite towns as cities developed further and expanded geographically. Cheap food imports caused many in agriculture to move into cities, and small factories in satellite towns were giving way to large companies in cities, which further increased population concentration in cities. Therefore the great metropolis became the hub of industrial society. Prior to 1848, "Berlin, Vienna, St. Petersburg, and Moscow in Europe, New York, Chicago, and Philadelphia in the United States, Buenos Aries and Rio de Janeiro in South America, and Tokyo, Calcutta, and Osaka in Asia, all surpassed the million mark" in population (Barraclough, in Wright, 1976: 164). The significant fact is that the emergence of great metropolitan centers was worldwide, and this phenomenon was not isolated to Europe. Industrialism of late-nineteenth-century imperialism also revolutionized the social structure of industrial society and rapidly integrated the world both economically and financially by the close of the nineteenth century. Even though this massive continuous development took place within the life span of one generation, it does not mean that all states and cities within them were developing at the same rate. Canadian, Australian, and Japanese industrialization lagged far behind other states in 1900. Equally important is that the Industrial Revolution had created a massive gap between the developed world and the underdeveloped world, which set the basis for exploitation of underdeveloped territories. British politician, social reformer, businessman, and ardent imperialist Joseph Chamberlin said, "The day of small nations has long passed away; the day of empires has come" (Wright, 1976: 169). This reflected the "new imperialism" in which there was an obsession with grandeur in the new world of sprawling cities and towering machines.

The Western world is now in a new revolution, that of the communications revolution. Just as the steam engine of the Industrial Revolution altered all aspects of the domestic and global economy and society and politics, electronic communication technology is changing today's industrial structure and organization, as well as the workplace, and it's causing many ripple effects of a questionable type, such as the accentuation of social inequalities within countries and the growing gap between the haves and the have-nots. As was the case during the Industrial Revolution, we find ourselves having difficulty in adapting to this new and rapid technological change because the technology of the communication age is in place, but the social institutions and value system that are to support it still lag behind.

Industrialization and Urbanization

According to Gideon Sjoberg (1965), the first cities came to being some 5,500 years ago; however, the human population that concentrated in cities did not begin to increase significantly until approximately one hundred years ago (130 years ago as of 2016). What permitted cities to evolve to a point where the masses could be accommodated? Each phase of urban evolution is characterized by its own technological, economic, social, and political patterns. The first phase of urban evolution and the least complex is the folk society, which is preurban and preliterate. The second phase is now called preindustrial feudal society, characterized by improved agricultural production and distribution, the use of reading and writing, and simple technology, such as sail ships and other technologies using kinetic energy. The third phase in the evolution of cities is the modern industrial city, characterized by mass literacy, an evident class structure, and major technological breakthroughs in the use of resources and energy that produced (and still sustain) the Industrial Revolution.

On the eve of the Industrial Revolution, Europe was still a predominantly agrarian society. It was the Industrial Revolution that brought about truly far-reaching changes in city life. Industrialism permitted and still permits people to live in cities because of vast improvements in agricultural farming techniques and food preservation to feed the masses, improved transportation and communications, and improved water supplies and effective sewage disposal. Today, nearly 80 percent of the people in the United Kingdom live in cities, as do 70 percent in the United States (Sjoberg, 1965). The preindustrial civilized world certainly did not have these kinds of urban population concentrations; only a small, socially dominant minority lived in cities. The colonial expansion of European power into other continents and the development of a technology based on natural resources and machinery, rather than human muscle, induced growth of cities in Asia, in parts of Africa, and in the Americas. This raised the standard of living in Europe and made possible the support of specialists, such as the scientist. The knowledge accumulated with the application of the scientific method is certainly one factor that made the modern city possible and permitted the human population to significantly concentrate in cities only 130 years ago.

Urbanization refers to the switch from a dispersed pattern of human settlement to one of concentration in urban areas. According to internationally recognized American sociologist and demographer Kingsley Davis (1965), "the only real source for the growth in the proportion of people in urban areas during the industrial transition was rural-urban migration." Rural-to-urban migration occurred because of the rise in technological enhancement of human productivity and certain constant factors. One constant factor is that manufacturing, commerce, and services were located in cities and could pay higher wages to former agricultural workers, who were faced with higher costs of agricultural production stemming from the introduction of costly technology and the need for less manpower. This scenario has repeated itself in every country that has passed through the Industrial Revolution. Advanced nations have now reduced their rate of urbanization; however, it is the underdeveloped world nations, representing three-fourths of humanity, that are mainly responsible for increasing urbanization of the world. Advanced nations' urbanization is witnessing a trend that now favors lower urban population densities because of suburbanization and population influxes into exurbia. This demonstrates that the territory covered by cities is growing faster than the population; in fact, cities can spread out so much that they practically connect physically with other cities, thus creating the polynucleated city. Population densities in a polynucleated scenario begin to increase once again because space for expansion runs out and human multiplication continues. The reason for presenting the trend toward polynucleated cities is to demonstrate the huge physical area that cities can occupy on earth and the huge number of people that reside in them. Science and technology has made this possible, but it cannot be overlooked that there are associated shortfalls.

Urban Economics and the Environment

Based on the discussion above, it becomes apparent how important cities have become in the Western world. Cities not only consume large geographic areas because of urban sprawl but also concentrate 70–80 percent of nations' populations. What do these large population concentrations mean, and what are the associated implications? Certainly one side effect of urbanization is that people increasingly choose to live in less densely populated neighborhoods, or in the country when income permits. This consumes space because it invokes urban sprawl and sets the scenario that could bring forth polynucleated city growth, as discussed above. What else does urbanization imply? For one thing, because Western world nations are highly urbanized, most human activity takes place in cities, whether in the central core, the city's fringe areas, suburbia and exurbia, or in tourist destinations such as towns like St. Sauveur, Québec. The fact that anthropogenic daily activity of all sorts, be it personal or commercial or industrial, occurs over the entire urban gradient, it is geographically concentrated mass activity that is sustained in every imaginable way by the natural environment.

Shortly after the American Great Depression, it was the government that stimulated capitalism once again with social and economic intervention. The government policies used to kick-start the economy were based on a theory developed by John Maynard Keynes, who left his mark on modern economic thought. Keynes was very interested in the social and political situation and viewed economic theory as a way to influence and create policy. In order to determine the type of government intervention that should take place to stimulate the economy of the times, Keynes changed his focus of study from microeconomics to macrolevel economic variables, and from this he introduced his economic approach and solution: "additional investment will always increase employment, and thus increase the total level of income, which will in turn lead to higher demand for consumer goods. In this way, investment stimulates economic growth and increases national wealth, which will eventually 'trickle down' to the poor" (Capra, 1983: 211). This Keynesian model did not take into account whether or not the process would achieve full employment or help the poor; the model simply assumed it would lead toward full employment and good for all, depending on external economic, social, and political factors. The implementation of the Keynesian trickle-down theory explains the key role of marketing and advertising as a way for the corporate world to manage demand in the marketplace. For the system to work, consumers are expected to continually increase their personal expenditures in the wider economy and in a predictable manner. In the twentieth century, the Keynesian model became ingrained into the mainstream of economic and political thought; this entails economic growth. It has contributed to creating our consumeristic and material-oriented culture. In fact, in capitalist, communist, and former communist economies, there is an addiction with growth factor. Economic and technological growth are seen as a must by almost all economists and politicians. This is the reason for all the hype bombarded on us involved with the selling of a lifestyle and its associated goods and services. It is clear, however, that continued growth in a finite natural environment will lead to very concerning environmental problems. The key ideology in government, business, and society is that maximization of progress and material wealth for individuals, groups, and institutions will be good for the common good. This reductionist view basically says that what is good for companies in industries such as railway, fast food, communications, computers, oil, mining, or automotive is good for Canada or the United States.

It is apparent that this view is not necessarily true because mass consumerism has taken its toll on Western society and will continue ruining the natural environment. The scary fact is that there now exists a global obsession with growth. Imagine the environmental pressures when the Soviet Union reaches full economic prosperity, or when populous China or developing nations reach their full capacities! Excessive consumption means continual degradation of quality of life and the natural environment in which we live. The new significance of urban areas, then, is that political ideologies highly linked to economic growth, consumerism, and mass marketing of products and lifestyles takes place in and primarily for people residing in highly populated urban areas, with television and radio commercials, promotional material on the Internet, billboards, print media, word of mouth, and psychological conformity sending the message to the urban consumer. Hence, consumption takes place in urban areas and continues to fuel the vortex of supply and demand, which causes depletion of nonrenewable resources and environmental degradation. This way of thinking and the associated consequences have now gone global. I will further investigate in parts 2 and 3 why and how globalization has occurred.

In Western society, competition and the notion of "survival of the fittest" have been the propellant of the economy and are the focal ideology of the corporate world. Hard work and success means individuals and entire families are allowed material well-being and consumption, and thus more economic growth takes place. What are some of the environmental and social impacts associated with increasing consumption and economic growth? To begin, it is important to state that all living things eventually die. The earth, understood as a living organism, is alive and in the process of continual natural degradation. The sun is expected to die, therefore no longer providing vital insolation required on earth to drive ecological systems. Although the death of our planet is inevitable, it will take many billions of years for this to materialize, allowing the planet to accommodate thousands of generations of humans. The scary fact is that anthropogenic activities may devastate the earth before it is time and ultimately cause the extinction of the human species and other life forms. Imagine that most of the environmental problems understood and experienced today have resulted from anthropogenic activity of only the last 130 years! Society must find ways to curtail this rapid trend, or else humankind's experience on earth may become more of a struggle and more limited in time.

As we have acknowledged already, the mechanistic Cartesian worldview has had a powerful influence on all sciences and on the Western way of thinking. Our linear, reductionist way of looking at nature and life is deeply ingrained in our culture, and therefore excessive growth has created a Western civilization that has caused the environment to respond in ways that are physically and mentally unhealthy for humans and other living species. Aside from environmental and health problems that are known, more invisible or camouflaged dangerous effects have been discovered recently and are still not fully comprehended. Even if one doesn't take into account the threat of nuclear disaster from bombs originating from enemies, human error, technological problems, or unstable governments, the global ecosystem and further evolution of life on earth are endangered due to substantial negative ecological impact. Big cities such as Los Angeles, Mexico City, Athens, and Istanbul, and where temperature inversions often occur (such as in Montreal), develop smog in the atmosphere, causing respiratory problems and skin and eye irritation for city inhabitants. For the environment, smog injures and kills plant life, and this can affect animal populations dependent on vegetation. Smog, which is caused by anthropogenic combustion of fossil fuels on earth, can also cause inadvertent global climatic change as human emissions from automobiles, factories, and other sources (such as aerosols) and human alterations made to the surface of the earth, including deforestation and urban development, are affecting the atmosphere's energy balance. This may result in a two- to three-degree Celsius increase in global temperatures. The implications of a warmer world climate are far-reaching, including the economy. Imagine the economic repercussions involved with a change in temperature that would affect such sectors as the tourism industry, the ski industry, or farming.

Another area of concern is municipal garbage disposal and terrestrial pollution, such as chemical waste dump sites that leak toxic liquids into neighboring bodies of water and produce toxic fumes that can cause birth defects, liver and kidney damage, respiratory problems, and various forms of cancer. Untreated industrially and domestically produced water emissions, alone or mixed synergistically, also threaten human health. Our massive dependency on oil-based products has led to oil-tanker traffic over our seas and rivers, and sometimes accidents cause huge amounts of oil spills, polluting tourist beaches and disrupting complex marine food webs. The generation of electricity from the burning of coal causes sulfur dioxide, nitrogen oxides, and other gases to be released into the air, which can cause cancer and medical problems for lungs. For the environment, sulfur and nitrogen oxide emissions from coal-burning power plants cause acid rain. Acid rain is produced because these gases mix with oxygen and water vapor in the atmosphere, and through chemical reactions they turn into sulfuric and nitric acids. These acids are then transported by wind, often across international boundaries, and fall to earth as acid rain or acid snow precipitation. Once acidic precipitation falls to earth, plant life is disturbed, agricultural and forest soils can be negatively impacted, and streams and lakes die because fish, insects, plants, and other forms of life cannot survive. Eastern Canada, eastern New England, and southern Scandinavia are heavily affected by acid rain as emissions emanating mostly from the southwestern United States are carried to these areas by westerly wind systems produced by the Coriolis effect, an inertial force that causes moving objects on the spherical rotating surface of the earth to deflect to the right in the northern hemisphere and to the left in the southern hemisphere. The deflection is greater near the poles and is smallest at the equator. An example is the firing of a cannonball. If fired to the north, the projectile will deflect to the east. It is the same with winds.

During the 1970s, the world became aware of how a shortage of fossil fuels can make economies and societies come to a standstill with the oil crisis. Leading industrialized countries embarked on finding new ways to provide energy. Some nations went as far as exploration of petroleum sources in the polar regions of the world, but decisions were made that would lead to the selection of nuclear power as an alternative energy source. Many nuclear accidents have already occurred, and major catastrophes have often been narrowly averted. The accidents at

Three Mile Island near Harrisburg, Pennsylvania, and at Chernobyl are prime examples. Associated with nuclear energy is the problem with disposal of nuclear waste generated by these power plants. There is no safe level of radiation. Radioactive by-products, especially plutonium, remain poisonous for at least half a million years. No human technology exists to safely store these residual products for a time period this long.

In considering fish stocks, one can grasp a better understanding of how much Western society really cares about the environment. It is clear that humanity often surpasses carrying capacities, which is the level at which humans maintain fish stocks to the level abundant to needs. This can cause a tragedy of the commons, meaning the overuse of a shared resource that is present for the common good of all users by depleting that resource. In recognition of a depleting resource base of fish, the Canadian government has been forced in the recent past to apply a moratorium on fishing in the Atlantic provinces until certain fish stocks replenish. This policy cost the Canadian public millions because it financially supported and retrained fishermen who were out of work. The worst thought, however, is there are not enough fish in the sea! Technology has given humans the upper hand in fishing. Frankly, the fish don't stand a chance because high-tech radar systems are used to track schools of fish, and technologies such as super nets that run many miles across oceans are intended to catch as many fish as possible.

Another issue is the steady decrease of the ozone layer, which protects all forms of life on earth from hazardous solar radiation. This atmospheric layer is in the process of disintegration, and holes have appeared at the north and south poles. Increased cases of skin cancer are expected and may affect our activities under the sun, including the tourism industry. Already we are told to wear protective lotions. Ozone depletion may also impact plant life and crops. Of course, there are a multitude of other examples of detriment to the natural world that can be discussed, however on the whole, humanity must acknowledge and understand that our relationship to the ecosystem is very close. This is what allows us to live. This is what we have to deal with.

The decline of Western society is evidenced by the poor status of the nuclear family, stress, heart disease, cancer, AIDS, mental disorders, crimes of all sorts, attitude disorders of the young, suicides, alcohol and drug use, economic instability and insecurity, unemployment, poor distribution of wealth, rapidly depleting resource base, and a threatened natural environment. These are problems that are difficult to find solutions to because they are highly intertwined and are subject to cause and effect. These issues cannot be understood and resolved within the compartmentalized structure found in our society's governmental institutions and academic disciplines. These days, politicians are at a loss for finding approaches and solutions to problems they are confronted with on a daily basis. Measures taken to allocate money or Band-Aid approaches will not resolve the problems faced by Western society. It is in altering the underlying dynamics at work of current problems that we can find solutions, and this will translate into massive changes of our social institutions, morals, values, beliefs, and ideas. Quite frankly, our world politics need to catch up to the social and environmental ills of our time. There is a desperate need for more political will.

The Transformation of Western Civilization

There are many examples of civilizations rising and falling. Some fell because they did not take care of their topsoil. Prosperity for ancient Greece, Spain, and areas of North Africa fell in correlation to a loss of topsoil. With our knowledge today, we will probably not fall because of questions surrounding our topsoil, because we now know how to build and maintain this valuable resource. However, there are other matters that pose a threat for our civilization.

Capra (1983) describes how Western Civilization is in transformation, and yet many do not even realize it. Key social indicators have been evident in Western society over the last twenty to thirty years: a sense of abandonment; disillusionment; frustration; augmented levels in mental illness, violent crime, and social upheaval; and interest in religious cultism. In times of historic cultural change, these types of parameters tend to appear ten to thirty years before the actual cultural transformation. Once the transformation is complete, such indicators fall in frequency. It appears that all civilizations go through a cyclical process. First they rise and grow, then they break down, and finally they disintegrate. After civilizations reach a peak in vigor, they have a tendency to lose their cultural vitality and decline. This happens because of a loss of flexibility from established rigid social structures and behavior patterns that cannot adapt to changing situations. During the process of decline, society's ability to respond to challenges is not completely lost because although the cultural mainstream still holds on to fixed ideas and rigid patterns of behavior, fringe groups (a source of creative thought) are born, culturally adapt, and propel the transformation. These fringe groups can be considered as a subculture of the mainstream culture; here I am referring to groups such as the anti-war movement, environmentalist groups, the feminist movement, and the like.

This discussion is representative of the situation taking place in Western society today, because there are three major transitions occurring at the same time that will affect our lives and our social, economic, and political systems. The first transition taking place is the slow decline of men as the central figure in civilization. The second is the decline of the fossil fuel age. The third is a sharp shift in thought taking place in our values, beliefs, and perception that shape our reality of today.

The scientific revolution, the period of enlightenment, and the Industrial Revolution (an era in world history that will be positioned as a very short period) shaped our values into belief in the scientific method as the only way of understanding nature; the view of the universe as a mechanical system; the view of life in society as a competitive struggle for existence; and the belief in unlimited progress and material well-being to be achieved through economic and technological growth. Baconian and Cartesian-Newtonian thinking is still prevalent today. An example of linear, reductionist thinking is that our society still believes in male-domineering, aggressive, expanding, competitive, "winning" activity over action that is more female conscious of the environment and life, is holistic, is intuitive, and provides a less or nonintellectual experience of reality. Society favors logic more than intuition and wisdom, science more than religion, competition more than cooperation, and exploitation of the natural environment more than conservation. This "winning" attitude and illusion of indefinite growth is headed by men as the center of civilization and Judeo-Christian tradition, which supports the views that man can dominate nature and women and that the rational mind plays a superior role than more nonintellectual ways of thinking. The Judeo-Christian tradition believes in the image of God as a male with unchallenged and definitive reason and power who rules the world from the heavens by imposing his godly law on it. Hence, our Western culture has attitudes and values that promote and reward masculine or self-assertive elements of human nature, and that disregard the feminine or intuitive aspects. All of this, perhaps inadvertently, is what Westerners are in the process of slowly changing in thought and actions. New cultural and economic norms that we are currently not very familiar with are slowly emerging—for better or for worse.

Whether or not we like it, we are in the process of decline and of transformation into a new civilization, but we cannot be certain that we will even complete the transformation because in just the last 130 years, humanity has altered or is in the process of altering the ecological systems that support life. The changes we are undergoing today may be more dramatic and amplified than prior ones because the pace of change is faster, more far-reaching, and more global than ever before.

As stated earlier, culture value shifts are occurring at the same time as the decline of men as the central figure in our culture and the decline of the Fossil Fuel Age. We are therefore, in Capra's terms, reaching the turning point.

Cultural transformations of this magnitude and depth cannot be prevented. They should not be opposed but, on the contrary, should be welcomed as the only escape from agony, collapse, or mummification. What we need, to prepare ourselves for the great transition we are about to enter, is a deep re-examination of the main premises and values of our culture, a rejection of those conceptual models that have outlived their usefulness, and a new recognition of some of the values discarded in previous periods of our cultural history. Such a thorough change in mentality of Western culture must naturally be accompanied by a profound modification of social relationships and forms of organization by changes that will go far beyond the superficial measures of economic and political readjustment being considered by today's political leaders.

Capra, 1983: 33

In the upcoming chapter, there will be a discussion concerning developing and underdeveloped nations' development, as well as problems that show the diffusion of Western thinking to these areas has created a mirror image of the Western world.

Part II

The Underdeveloped World within Us: The Case of Latin America

Chapter 4

The Mirror Image of the West

Colonialism, Urbanization, and Dependency

In part 2 we will investigate the tragedies taking place in areas of the third world. Many often ask why the underdeveloped world is in such poverty, or even, why poverty exists. In this section, an attempt is made to clarify the causes and effects of the development of underdevelopment. The gap between industrial nations and underdeveloped nations is getting wider, and this trend is confirmed in statistics that show:

> ... developed market economy countries (primarily Western and southern Europe, North America, and Japan) account for only 20% of the world's population and yet accumulate 68% of the world's total GNP. In contrast, the 47% of the world's population which lives in developing market economy countries (the non-socialist Third World) receives only 12% of the total GNP. Ignoring the type of economic system for the moment, we find that 70% of the world's population who live in developing countries receive only 16% of the total GNP whereas the 30% who inhabit the developed countries receive 84% of the total GNP. Seventy-five percent of the world's people live at levels well below the U.S. poverty line and receive only 21% of the world GNP.
>
> Abu-Lughod and Hay, 2007: 85–88

The Development of Underdevelopment

European colonialism wasn't simply a significant cause of urban growth and industrialization in the Western world; it also had massive implications for the countries that were colonized. One can say that European colonialism created third world underdevelopment and continues to perpetuate it in the countries of Latin America, Africa, and Asia. Many of the countries we now consider developing or underdeveloped had their own economies prior to colonialism, with populations that had lived in accordance with their own technologies, resources, and social and cultural structures; even urban areas existed.

Nonetheless, the period of European colonialism highly influenced the course of development of these nations, and today we acknowledge the devastating results, such as poverty, squatter settlements, unhealthy living conditions, indebtedness, and so on. Although colonialism lasted until the early twentieth century, a new form of colonialism still persists and is contributing to keeping the have-nots in perilous conditions. In understanding how underdevelopment took place, the focus of this next section will be on the Latin American experience during and after initial colonialism, but it should be viewed as being generally representative of other regions now considered developing or underdeveloped. The context in which this discussion will be pursued is that of dependency theory.

André Gunder Frank, a German-American economic historian and sociologist, believes that we cannot develop adequate development theory and policy for the three-quarters of the world's population living in underdeveloped conditions without first understanding their historical economic and social situations that brought forth their current underdevelopment (Frank, 1969: 3–16). Our ignorance about the underdeveloped countries' history leads us to assume that their history and present situation resemble earlier stages of the history of our now developed countries. In virtually no way does the past or present of underdeveloped countries resemble the past of the now developed countries. Developed countries were really never underdeveloped, although they may have been undeveloped. Contemporary underdevelopment is caused in large part by the historical past and continuing economic and other relations between the satellite countries (those underdeveloped) and metropolitan countries (those developed). These relations are largely responsible for the structure and development of the capitalist system on a worldwide scale. The expansion of the capitalist system over the past centuries penetrated every aspect of the underdeveloped world, and therefore the economic, political, social, environmental, and cultural institutions and relations present are the results of the historical development of the capitalist system.

According to Frank (1969), on a worldwide scale capitalism produces a core of developed countries and an underdeveloped periphery of countries. This same process can also be found in the internal economic structure of peripheral nations in which domestically, a metropolis (for example, a capital city or major city) produces an underdeveloped satellite (peripheral regions or surrounding satellite cities). With these scenarios in mind, it is apparent that the role of major cities in the third world was and still is the instrument of world capitalistic domination. The process involved is one of third world dependency upon core nations in which domestic peripheral areas furnish strategic domestic cities, who in turn supply core countries. Proof of the fact that peripheral nations are dependent on core nations and suffer because of this is the fact that peripheral nations experience their greatest economic development and industrial development if and when ties to core countries are weakest, especially seen in times of the World Wars and the Great Depression. When core countries recover from crisis and reestablish trade and investment ties, the previous development and industrialization of peripheral nations is impeded or guided in directions that are not self-perpetuating. This was evident in Argentina, India, and Brazil after World War II, when America resumed its economic invasion. The regions most underdeveloped today are those that had the closest ties to the core countries in the past. Once peripheral nations could no longer supply core nations wealth from their mines, or the market for sugar disappeared, the existing economic, political, and social structure of these regions prohibited autonomous economic development and left them to fall into underdevelopment. This trend was evident even in the sixteenth century, when integration into the European economy favored commodity circulation and undermined the self-sufficiency of local agrarian structures in Latin America (Roberts, 1981: 38).

Colonialism and Urbanization

As mentioned earlier, cities in the third world were developing prior to colonialism, but eventually more regional cities developed, were conquered, and were used to fan capitalistic intentions. It is because of colonialism that Latin American cities took on certain characteristic features. First of all, there wasn't a large concentration of inhabitants because most still lived in rural areas. There existed disorderliness, filth, and poverty of the majority of the population; however, those in the upper echelons dressed well, were cultured, and noticeably consumed colonial wealth in excess. The urban economy also had a large service sector providing employment in entertainment, shopping, and domestic service. All these economic traits were oriented toward the colonial city's major role, that of political and administrative power, which was the geographic area where organization and control of its peripheral commercial agriculture and mining took place. Bryan Roberts states, "In Latin America towards the end of the colonial period ... poor interregional communications and a weakly developed or non-existent interregional division of labour meant that commercial and landed interests of the difficult regions depended on the political and administrative power of their local city" (1981: 43). The profits of the colonial economy were forwarded through the urban centers to government, merchants, and the Church.

Increasing integration into the European economy in the nineteenth century changed the pattern of urbanization in Latin America. The factors involved in these changes were: (a) new technologies from industrialized Europe at highly competitive costs, (b) new forms of transport that lowered the costs of carrying goods overseas or land, and, (c) the Industrial Revolution in Europe and its associated growth of urban populations, which created a new and expanding demand for nonprecious minerals and foodstuffs that could be produced in the tropics and temperate areas of the world. The dominant trend in the urbanization of Latin America in the nineteenth century was the increasing importance of regional cities. The degree of importance of a city was dependent on the extent of their connection with the world economy: the more exports a city had, the more important it became, and the higher the population that concentrated in the regional cities. By 1920, most Latin American countries had important regional cities. Therefore foreign investments, especially by the British, were implemented in a manner that promoted the importance of certain cities by helping to provide the administrative and economic infrastructures for exports, and the major city became a channel for export. The American contribution was less significant at this time; however, they received export materials and in return imported manufactured products that were consumed in the major cities. In other areas of Latin America at this time, such as in Venezuela and Columbia, due to their weak incorporation into the world economy and poor internal transport, growth of nodal cities was impeded. The manner in which capitalism diffused overseas produced economic and social backwardness in the local population because of the continuance of archaic institutions and uneven development in which nodal, export-oriented cities existed alongside stagnant peripheries and provincial economies.

Roberts (1981) explains how in the twentieth century, urban industrialization has become the dominant economic force in Latin America, slowly eroding the importance of the rural agricultural sector. One reason for increased Latin American industrial growth in the twentieth century is foreign investment that began to concentrate in manufacturing. For example, between 1912 and 1929, thirty-two US companies opened operations in Brazil (Roberts, 1981: 64). A second reason that promoted industrialization was the fact that external events, particularly the Great Depression and two World Wars, stimulated local production of required industrial materials. In addition, during the first half of the twentieth century, it became apparent in Latin American countries that it was not wise to depend solely on the export of primary products as competition for the same Latin American products grew from other underdeveloped areas, which were closely aligned under the control of the colonial powers. The fact that the developed world created chemical industries that began to replace the demand for natural fibers and nitrates also contributed significantly; this was closely associated with the fact that Western markets needed stable supplies. Also, the European powers and the United States adopted more stringent commercial policies, notably tariff and quota systems that would close huge markets to Latin American products. The social forces produced by the development of the export economy in the nineteenth century gave further reason to industrialize as foreign interests and workers restricted the performance of native enterprise and caused limitations in social mobility. Finally, industrialism in countries of Latin America that were highly integrated into the world economy by the beginning of the twentieth century was pursued because nationalism and state intervention promoted industrialization, and one of the aims was to reduce dependence on foreign markets. Hence, social, economic, and political forces in the early twentieth century established a foundation for industrialization. The types of industries established in the first part of the century were oriented toward simplistic consumer goods, such as tools and construction materials, textiles, basic pottery, food and beverages, wood processing, and glassware. These businesses were characterized as being small-scale and promoted by local capital, which spurred industrialization and the creation of local employment opportunities in the manufacturing sector.

By the 1940s, some countries such as Mexico, Argentina, and Brazil moved into an advanced stage of industrialization, producing rubber, steel, cement, and petroleum. From 1925 to 1950, factories and artisan production used part of the workers migrating to cities from rural areas. It became increasingly apparent, however, that there were identifiable problems in the economies of Latin American countries, which would deflate the spin-off effects of industrialization. By 1956, it was evident that people migrating to cities were increasingly absorbed into the service sector and marginal activities, which served to depress productivity. Also, the vast growth of small-scale, inefficient workshops based on the ample supply of cheap labor from rural areas contributed to diminishing industrial spin-offs. An underdeveloped agricultural sector and the slow progress of industrialization created a poor employment situation. By the 1960s, there was a disappointing performance in increasing industry employment opportunities. By the mid-1960s, technologically advanced facilities required less manpower. Mass poverty therefore created a situation in which Latin American countries' industrial and market expansion were inhibited.

The Colonialism of New Dependency

Brazilian economist and professor Theotonio Dos Santos explains that after the Second World War, a new dependency of Latin American nations on advanced nations was created in response to the changing needs of the Western economy. The developed countries' needs continually change, and therefore economic imperialism takes on transformation over time. For example, the first phase of British economic imperialism to affect Latin America was different from that of the more recent American economic imperialism. These transformations set the stage in which the conditions of exchange between advanced nations and underdeveloped nations can either promote or limit development within underdeveloped countries. The new dependency of underdeveloped nations is based on capital-intensive investments by multinational corporations; Dos Santos labels this a technological-industrial dependency. This type of dependency has placed limits on the development of Latin American economies. Urban industrialization in underdeveloped countries has not reduced dependence on advanced nations because industrialization has caused an increase in the amount of foreign control and participation in these economies. Hence, underdeveloped or developing countries have not had an independent economic development. Their development and present economic condition is closely tied to the economic development of the advanced capitalist world (Dos Santos, 1970: 232).

In the twentieth century, American investments have dealt with industrial production in the underdeveloped world; over time the Americans have shifted their economic activity from extractive industries to manufacturing and technologically advanced products, such as durable consumer goods. There were many changes in advanced capitalist economies that prompted this pattern of industrial urbanization in Latin America and other underdeveloped countries:

a) After World War II, and partly because of technological advancements made during that war, the most advanced capitalist economies accelerated their rate of technological innovation. Underdeveloped countries provided a limited market for these goods and could be sold only where there was a concentrated high income population;

b) The increase of technological innovation and the potential to sell these innovations in underdeveloped parts of the world led developing nation companies and multinationals to a transfer of capital to underdeveloped areas so that production of goods could take place there using cheap labor rates. This allowed profitable production;

c) Local production could not compete with advanced technology introduced by advanced capitalism, and therefore this opened up less advanced markets. The tendency that has emerged is that advanced capitalist countries keep the most productive economic activities for themselves (like computers) and direct routine production to poorer countries, where costs of production are usually lower;

d) These capital-intensive investments for multinationals are worthwhile only when there is an internal market for their goods and a possibility offering the opportunity in which underdeveloped countries may export the industrial products of the multinationals to other countries. For example, the Brazilian automobile industry exports to all of Latin America because there is a profitable market for the multinational car maker compared to direct export from the mother country, where costs of production and transport are higher.

Roberts, 1981: 76–81

This form of industrialization is directed to the few cities of the underdeveloped or developing world where middle- and upper-income groups are existent and can purchase consumer goods. Scarcity of capital in underdeveloped nations has contributed to a lack of diversification and expansion in the industrial structure of countries; therefore, the easiest way for governments to stimulate industrialization has been to rely on capital investment from multinationals through the use of technology that is increasingly popular among the targeted consumers of underdeveloped nations. The products of advanced technology sell well in underdeveloped countries because higher income groups can afford them, and because these groups have adopted consumption patterns very similar to those found in the Western world. The governments of the less developed world have encouraged foreign investment through subsidies, tax incentives, and lenient environmental controls. All these factors perpetuate economic dependence and contribute to the stagnation of provincial regions because the focus of foreign business and local government attention and development is on stimulating growth in a few large cities. This also perpetuates poor distribution of wealth both geographically and socially.

The Case of Malnutrition: Brazil

The discussion continues by focusing on one aspect that was mentioned earlier concerning the consumption patterns that underdeveloped countries have adopted from the Western world. To demonstrate the enormous impact Western influence is having on such nations, the following discussion will focus solely on the subject of malnutrition in Brazil. At first glance with dependence on the standards used in calculating per capita calorie consumption, one may infer that calorie requirements to sustain individuals is sufficient in Brazil. Unfortunately, this is not the case. Statistics provided by Knight (1979: tables 14–15) show that caloric deficits existed in all regions of Brazil except the rural southeast. It is estimated that 32.8 percent of the total population met full FAO/WHO low calorie requirements in 1975, almost 18.6 percent had small deficits of up to 200 calories, another 31.3 percent had moderate deficits in the 200–400 calorie range, and 17.3 percent had deficits above 400 calories. Faced with malnourishment figures of this type, one can deduce that the effects of malnourishment are long lasting and will haunt Brazilian society and development. Eveleth (1976: 1) states that using physical and mental conditions of children is the best means of attaining a good idea of the nutritional status of a population. The literature continuously shows that malnutrition is strongly affected by income, and thus it is likely that less affluent groups of children will suffer the most nutrition related consequences. Physically, it has been found in studies of working and lower-class children in Sao Paulo that those of low and high class groups were close to the FAO/WHO weight standard at the age of three months. The weight of low-paid white collar and manual workers' children in slum areas was below standards by age twelve. In comparison, a Porto Alegre study indicated that height and weight of preschool children from wealthy families are above FAO/WHO standards, compared to children from less affluent origins (Costa, 1970). At the mental level, a child's mental capacity to learn is dependent on good nutrition at early stages of life and on family income. The less family income, the less chance an individual has in contributing to the development of the nation due to physical or mental incapacities. Nutritional deficiency is an associated cause of infective and parasitic diseases, which causes the death of many children of the age of five years or under. Diseases such as kwashiorkor, marasmus, and rickets are common in Brazil (deBlij, 1977: 64). Hence, malnourishment of this type contributes to widening the gap between rich and poor Brazilians.

It is often asked why there is enough food produced in the world for all its inhabitants, but there are still many people lacking the proper nutrition. The answer not only lies in lack of money to purchase foods but also with the interrelated web of food consumption, production, distribution, and national and international factors. In general, two broad types of limitations on food consumption and nutrition can be discussed. The first has to do with quantity, and the other with quality.

Limitations of Food Quantity

Brazil's industrial development has been accompanied by a regressive distribution of wealth, which accounts for a significant part of malnourishment of those located in particular regions of Brazil and its cities. Certainly a lack of money for people of these areas causes them to have deficient diets, but why is it that these segments of the population lack adequate amounts of money to buy food? In general, unemployment is one reason. In slum areas of major cities, migrants from rural areas, many of which have been forced off their lands by unfair means to accommodate agribusiness, are left unemployed due to lack of job opportunities offered by cities (Arroyo, 1976: 266). Their plight is usually because in regions such as the northeast, government policies have permitted the displacement of so-called uneconomical small farm operations to the interior of the country—or their elimination—and have allowed the influx of larger, mechanized farms either of a local nature or multinational nature linked with agro-industries and foreign markets. Agro-industries have taken hold of the bulk of agricultural production, which decreases employment demands. As Arroyo states, "rural unemployment increases fastest in those areas that modernize agriculture" (1976: 268). The technology transfer from the Western Green Revolution, which has been implemented by agribusiness in areas such as Brazil, has been undeniably profitable for agribusiness, but it has not been advantageous for the underdeveloped world.

> The industrial nations are increasingly interested in penetrating the agricultures of the underdeveloped countries and have lately found new ways and means to achieve this end. This penetration, even if one assumes that it is not a deliberate strategy to forestall agrarian reforms and other structural changes of benefit to the rural masses, will most certainly have this result ... The Green Revolution is far more than the propagation of excellent seeds: it subjects the underdeveloped agricultures to an economic and political control which may result from the transfer of technology; and by the same token, it is, and is meant to be, a world-wide counter-reform program ... Thus the almost incredible phenomenon occurs under our very noses that a "program destined to feed the peoples of the world" causes larger unemployment, great poverty, and more hunger in the rural sector.
>
> Ernest Feder, 1975

> The West has tried to apply its own conceptions of "development" to the Third World, working through local elites and pretending that the benefits showered on these elites would trickle down to the less fortunate, especially through the wholesale application of Western-inspired and Western-supplied technology. These methods have not produced a single independent and viable economy in the entire Third World—and in fact were not meant to. "Development" has been the password for imposing a new kind of dependency, for enriching the already rich world and for shaping other societies to meet its commercial and political needs.
>
> Susan George, 1976

Another factor limiting caloric quantity is the role of agribusiness and the export economy. Professor Homen de Malo from the University of Sao Paulo comments in a 1984 LARR report (RB-84-06) that "the expansion of farming lands used for export (soybeans, oranges, cotton, peanuts, tobacco, and sugar cane), is forcing a drop in cultivation of basic foods for domestic consumption." What de Malo forgets to stress is that during the 1980s this situation helped pay for Brazil's 105-billion-dollar debt through export earnings, but it decreased the supply of food internally and therefore elevated food prices for the population. This resulted in the decrease of nutritious food consumption for low-income earners. Finally, the Brazilian government's general development strategy and monetary policies also affected people's capacity to purchase foods. Economic policies carried out by the military regime since 1964 focused on building an effective modern industrial infrastructure, and they neglected the expansion of social services, such as public health, sanitation, education, and housing. As a result, one consequence of such policy was the cut in real wages of the middle class. An LARR report (RB-84-05:3) stressed the fact that middle-class persons earning up to thirty times the minimum wage saw their pay reduced to only fifteen times the minimum wage. The major implication of this type of wage policy was that it worked against people's purchasing power. According to the same LARR report, the true objective of such a wage policy was not to fight inflation, as suggested by the IMF, but to create conditions in which Brazil could pay off its massive debt to advanced lender countries and international organizations such as the IMF and World Bank. Hence, in 1979 the minimum salary bought more beans, milk, soybean oil, and meat than it did in the early 1980s. Stated in another manner, in Sao Paulo, the richest area in Brazil, consumption of essential foods fell by 18 percent during the first five months of 1984 compared to the same time period in 1983 (LARR, RB-84-06:3). In sum, if government policies are negatively affecting more affluent people in more prosperous regions and cities of Brazil, how can the poor in economically depressed geographic regions and city slums have enough money to buy an abundance of nutritious foods? There is evidence that suggests all poverty-stricken Brazilians were cooking and eating less; at that time, estimates put Brazil's undernourished at 35 million (LARR, RB-84-06).

Limitations of Food Quality

International factors affect consumption in both a direct and indirect fashion. The integration of Brazil into the world economy has been highly influenced by multinational corporations of all sorts entering its state boundaries. The result has been that mainly American multinationals have dominated many sectors of the economy. In so doing, multinationals from the soft drink and fast-food industries have also affected the nutritional quality of foods ingested by Brazilians because of an increasing shift in Brazilian culture, values, and beliefs. Knight (1979: 70) refers to the fact that there is a relatively low proportion of total family expenditure devoted to food purchases in metropolitan areas and other urban areas compared to rural localities. This fact comes as no surprise because the demonstration effect is most prevalent in metropolitan areas. The demonstration effect is imposed on Brazilians by multinationals who effectively market and advertise durable goods and foods normally consumed in the Western world. Their marketing and advertising strategies are so good that they stimulate wants and needs within the Brazilian population through television, radio, print advertising, signs, and billboards. The demonstration of Western products and foods has lured many Brazilians away from usual local consumption patterns and has negatively influenced what they now eat. Knight (1979: 79) offers the example of inadequate feeding of infants: he states that breast-feeding is declining in urban Brazil due to the introduction of commercial milk-based baby formulas developed by multinationals. After approximately six weeks of weaning their child, mothers turn to baby formulas, which are often overdiluted and served unhygienically. The overdilution and hygiene factors are the result of family income limitations. The result is that children do not receive good nutrition, and thus many suffer from malnutrition and many of its related consequences—or they die. The child mortality rate in Brazil during the first half of the 1980s was two hundred deaths per one thousand born (LARR, RB-84-06:3). Fortunately, this figure has improved. Since 1996, this number has leveled-off to 16 deaths per one thousand for infants under the age of five years (The World Bank, 2016). The reasons for this improvement are explained in the next paragraphs.

The selling of the North American consumeristic lifestyle and nutrition is being felt in other ways as well. For instance, besides avoiding more local nutritious foods, Brazilians are buying costly consumer durables, thus avoiding purchases of abundant and nutritious foods (Knight, 1979: 71). An example of this is the notion of a Brazilian buying a fashionable product such as a refrigerator but not having enough money to fill it up with food! The powerful demonstration effect discussed above, coupled with the cultural avoidance of certain foods such as eggs, heighten malnutrition even more. Influential Brazilian elites who highly portray culture traits from advanced countries simply add to the problem of malnutrition as the masses copy allocentric groups and become even more inclined to "live like the Americans."

The great news in the case of Brazil is that the country provides a very good example of what can be achieved in the eradication of hunger if proper actions are taken, principally by governments possessing the strong will to do so. According to Holmes, Hagen-Zanker, and Vandemoortele (2011), as a developing middle-income nation, Brazil is one of the wealthiest countries in the world, and its GDP growth rate increased from 1.9 percent to 5.1 percent per annum between 1998 and 2008. According to Prableen Bajpai (2016), presently Brazil stands as the seventh largest economy in the world by measure of nominal GDP. It is certainly the largest economy in Latin America, worth $2.24 trillion (for comparative reasons, the leading nation in the world is the United States with an economy worth $17.41 trillion followed by China at $10.35 trillion, then Japan at $4.77 trillion, Germany at $3.82 trillion, United Kingdom at $2.99 trillion, France at $2.83 trillion; in eighth place is Italy with an economy worth $2.06 trillion, Russia at $2.05 trillion, and India in tenth place with an economy worth $2.04 trillion; Canada finds itself just out of tenth place with a dollar worth of $1.79 trillion). Nonetheless, Holmes, Hagen-Zanker, and Vandemoortele (2011) say that the country still has one of the highest rates of inequality in the world, and poverty levels are still considered high, with over 20 percent of the population (representing forty million people) living under the poverty line and 7 percent (thirteen million) being extremely poor. Between the early 1990s and 2008, levels of inequality and poverty were halved. Changes made by government during the same time period in legislation and implementation of related special programs oriented at income redistribution helped elevate the population's minimum wage and overall level of disposable income. They also permitted more public expenditures on health, education, and other social services, as well as the protection of such services. Since the early 1980s, the Brazilian government has instituted programs specific to the elimination of hunger and undernourishment. In fact, Carlo Augusto Monteiro (2009) states that the decline of child malnutrition has been impressive in Brazil compared to other parts of the developing world. He says that for children under five years of age in 1996 and in 2006–2007, severe forms of malnutrition were virtually eliminated throughout the country, including the northeast region. Brazil is now the leader of the developing world in regard to reduction of hunger and malnutrition. The situation with breast-feeding of infants has vastly improved in the last twenty years, as discussed by Khazan (2015), who says that more than 50 percent of Brazilian mothers exclusively breast-feed their infants until they are six months old, compared to 16 percent for American moms. Unlike the United States, Brazil and dozens of other countries have banned advertising or promotion of infant formula. Breast-feeding in public is now encouraged by the government, and in March 2015, the Sao Paulo municipal government passed a bylaw that fines businesses or organizations that inhibit mothers from breast-feeding in public. They also widely encourage mothers to eat healthy during the breast-feeding period.

The problem with the effort devoted to decreasing malnutrition and hunger is that Brazil presently faces a nationwide dilemma with obesity in its population, caused primarily by changes in lifestyle and eating habits resembling that of advanced Western economies. Eduardo J. Gomez (2012) states that these changes are heavily related to transnational corporations who have introduced the population to processed foods (yogurts, ice cream, chocolate, sugary soft drinks) and greasy fast foods, especially since the mid-1990s. This same journalist says that other reasons contributing to the problem of obesity are easy access to cheap foods; the increased use of computers, television, and the Internet; and the growth of sedentary jobs and associated longer work hours. This is the demonstration effect at its best. Gomez's article continues by saying that a survey conducted by the Ministry of Health found that the percentage of overweight persons increased from 42.7 percent in 2006 to 48.5 percent in 2011. With reference to obesity levels, the rate increased from 11.4 percent to 15.8 percent over the same time period, and these weight-related increases are the cause of diseases, such as type 2 diabetes, heart disease, and cancer, representing 41 percent of total health care costs. Bassi (2014) says that according to the World Food Programme, only 6.9 percent of Brazil's population is affected by hunger. The small percentage of those who do not have access to food live in isolated rural areas or indigenous communities, but the most serious problem now is obesity: 51 percent of the country's population and one in three children age five to nine is overweight. The quality of foods ingested is a problem, but so are the unregulated advertising practices associated with food products.

This discussion on malnutrition in Brazil has served to illustrate the far-reaching dissemination and influence of linear Western thinking in Latin America and the third world in general, and it is representative of more aspects than just nutrition. Just as the Western world is caught up in the vortex of the Keynesian economic model, which is dependent on consistent and predictable spending by consumers, the underdeveloped nations' governments and peoples are caught in a very similar vortex. In the process, people in less developed countries have been changing their values, ideas, and beliefs to resemble those of our Western culture. The penetration of the consumer ethic has trickled down from cities to small towns, villages, and rural areas in the third world and has helped to create "the impression of participating in the modern world portrayed by the images on the television screen" (Armstrong, 1985: 6). By extension, the race to industrialize their economies and live like the modern world further contributes to environmental problems. The open invitation governments of less developed nations have given to foreign companies to invest in their states reflects the notion of an "open sewer"—basically, very few environmental restrictions are imposed, and an array of attractive monetary incentives are offered to lure them there. At the social level, the race to industrialize their economies, and thus contribute to driving Western capitalism, exclude low-income populations from the benefits of economic growth. This is apparent when we consider that in many Latin American countries such as Mexico and Brazil, urban health, educational, and public service facilities are unevenly distributed because rich parts of cities are better serviced than low-income areas. The urban poor therefore continue to live in squatter settlements, where there exist malnutrition, unpaved roads, lack of abundant water supply, and lack of good sewage disposal. The exclusion of the poor from access to an acceptable income and public services causes their marginality in cities and the peripheral regions.

Part III

The Circumpolar North

Chapter 5

The North-South Dilemma

Introduction

In parts 1 and 2, we have investigated the causes and effects of the pattern of Western capitalist economic expansion and thinking. We have acknowledged how the underdeveloped world has been influenced by Western civilization and made dependent. Our next focus is on northern regions of the globe, known as the circumpolar north. This cold, remote region has also been absorbed into the sphere of influence of southern Western ideology and economic expansion. The ensuing discussion illustrates once again the impact of Western thought on communities now desperately struggling to retain some semblance of their history, heritage, tradition, and way of life in the face of manly aggressive influences from southern areas. Using a general perspective, it will be shown that just as Western ways of thinking have influenced the underdeveloped areas of the world, northern areas have also been afflicted. We are not just talking about southern intervention, but southern intervention of a particular kind. Despite their differences, the state and private enterprise serve to remove or limit native autonomy and foster dependence. This has led to many social and environmental issues and concerns.

Though the extent and size of the circumpolar north is not exactly known to date, in the past few decades, interested individuals have recorded the more explicit characteristics and the changes in them (Sater, 1969: 1–4). During the energy crisis of the early 1970s, our generation witnessed the extent to which our industrially dependent standard of living relied upon the natural environment for resources such as stored energy and hydroelectric power. The energy crisis opened the eyes of both the general public and governments. As a result, extensive searches for new sources of energy have been undertaken in order to improve and guarantee the economic vitality of North American, Western European, and former Eastern Bloc nations. Many state governments involved in seeking new sources of energy have found that the circumpolar north has a lot of untapped resources that are beneficial for southern economies. This does not imply that the circumpolar region of the world was left untouched by Americans or Europeans in the historical past; on the contrary, the circumpolar north was utilized for economic reasons. According to Muller-Wille and Pelto (1975: 2), "most of the circumpolar north was drawn into the orbit of European-American economic expansion over 200 years ago, though some of the interior regions of northern Canada, for example, were scarcely touched by the fur traders and other European entrepreneurs until well into the 19th century." The main factor now is that the exploitation of economic resources from the circumpolar north has increased tremendously since the time before industrialization (Hustich, 1972: 43). The 1960s in particular showed a marked penetration of southern interest directed at the exploitation of economic resources of the circumpolar north (Muller-Wille and Pelto, 1975: 5). In the future, the industrialists' quest for more economic resources is bound to intensify exploitation of the circumpolar areas of the world. As mentioned earlier, a number of interested individuals have recorded the changes taking place in the circumpolar north. Certainly these changes have been physical, but alterations in the human context have also taken place. Based on the literature referred to, there appears to be a marked correlation between the amount of resource exploitation taking place over time in the circumpolar north by southern intervention and the degree of impact on both the physical and human aspects of this region. This means that as southern interests have gradually and increasingly penetrated into circumpolar regions for economic reasons, impacts on the physical and human condition have also gradually and increasingly taken place.

Stages of Economic Development of the North

Hustich (1972: 43–44) states that the colonization of the circumpolar north by outsiders has developed differently in different parts of the northern zones. He emphasizes, however, that most of these zones have undergone three major eras of economic development.

In the initial era, the first colonizers saw that the economic base of northerners was mainly characterized by fishing, hunting, reindeer herding, and fur trading. This era lasted until the late 1800s. During this era, the lifestyles of the indigenous peoples of the circumpolar regions were not highly influenced by outsiders, mainly because of the way outsiders perceived the climatic environment of the north. Thus, natives maintained their established man-land relationships, localized subsistence economies, customary activities, and cultural and traditional values, lifestyles, and kinship ties (Muller-Wille and Pelto, 1975: 3).

The second era, which commenced around the turn of the twentieth century, proved to be an example of what was to come in later decades. During the second era, aboriginals of the circumpolar north experienced increased economic vibrancy mainly due to augmented levels of outside intervention. This era saw the beginnings of delocalization, which is defined as "the tendency for any territorially-defined population to become increasingly dependent on resources, information flow, and socio-economic linkages with the systems of energy and resources outside their particular area" (Pelto, 1975: 31).

According to Pelto (1975: 32), delocalization arose due to the intrusion of traders; settlers from the outside; missionaries; government agents; imported commodities such as guns, flour, and kerosene; and the introduction of a cash economy. As a result of the delocalization process, acculturation and transformations in indigenous life styles (such as mode of production) were on the rise.

The beginning of the third era of colonization, during the early 1960s, can be regarded as an intermediate step into the delocalization of human characteristics in the circumpolar region. This stage was marked by the increased dependency of the circumpolar natives on fuel resources from outside areas for snowmobiles and home heating purposes (Pelto, 1975: 32). The impact of the snowmobile on traditional ways of life for circumpolar peoples was studied by Ludger Muller-Wille, who found that among the Sami of Northwestern Finland, most young males considered themselves to be reindeer herders until the early 1960s. As the dependency on the snowmobile increased, male migration to more southern economic centers occurred due to the decreased need for reindeer herders (Muller-Wille, 1971: 271–287). During the 1960s, accelerated economic exchange between local populations and the economic systems of the wider world took place as most of the circumpolar regions were completely or nearly completely cash economies. Simultaneously, increased differentiation among indigenous peoples was apparent as some families managed to accumulate cash and machines, whereas others became dependent on welfare, unemployment benefits, and other cash support payments (Pelto, 1975: 33). Further, the presence of outside intervention was made even more explicit as mining operations resulted in the exploitation of coal in Svalbard and Vortuka, copper at Norilsk, gold at Great Bear Lake, and lead in Greenland (Hustich, 1972: 44). Certainly the depression of the 1930s and the ending of World War II provided increased international knowledge of northern resources and the technological means to overcome harsh climatic conditions. These factors contributed to increasing the delocalization process of the early 1960s.

The mid-1970s to the present represent the advanced stages of delocalization and economic development of the circumpolar north. This is reflected in the heavy northward flow of capital investments in projects such as the James Bay hydroelectric development in the Québec north, the Mackenzie Valley Alyeska gas pipeline project, and tourism development and planning (Mitchell and Sewell, 1981: 56). Along with this advanced stage comes the increasing transformations concerning increased population concentration in small settlements; shifts in traditional ways of life, cultures, and traditions; mode of production; and social organization of the circumpolar natives.

Impacts on Circumpolar Societies

According to Hustich (1972: 40), the circumpolar north is about nineteen million square kilometers and holds a small population of about fourteen million. Its more recent past has shown that it was integrated more physically than it was socially, economically, or politically. There has been political domination of the northlands due to increased southern economic and strategic military interest in past decades. In fact, the circumpolar north was once fragmented into west and east under the auspices of the capitalist and communist economic systems. Until recently, it was difficult to describe the circumpolar peoples as being one polar community. Even though the circumpolar north was divided between west and east, penetration of southern economics into these northern areas had and still has very similar human impacts on natives, even in the new scenario of the post–Cold War era.

One of the impacts felt throughout the circumpolar region is that of urbanization. As economic investments increasingly made their mark on the circumpolar landscape, the once nomadic northern populations left—or in many circumstances, they were relocated from their uneconomical ecological kinship mode of production (such as hunting, fishing, and agriculture) and concentrated in modern economic mining and industrial settlements. For instance, on the Kola Peninsula in the Soviet north, the degree of urbanization in this area was 89 percent during the 1960s and 1970s (Hustich, 1972: 44). Urbanization became rampant during the 1960s and

1970s: the population of the Northwest Territories was 80 percent urbanized; the Yukon was 70 percent, Alaska was 60 percent, the Laplands in Finland was 45 percent, and Iceland was 70 percent. These types of urbanization levels are evident throughout the entire north (Hustich, 1972: 45, table 3). Although at first glance, urbanization levels of this type look encouraging and represent living standards and lifestyles similar to our own, the northerner's experience in urban areas is not as comfortable as one might think. The shift from the kinship mode of production (hunting and gathering societies) to the modern cash economy found in northern urban areas—which provides higher incomes, modern housing, electricity, schools, nursing stations, and welfare checks—has been accompanied by changes in native cultures and traditional ways of life and the natural environment. For example, with respect to work opportunity for natives in northern Canada, Waltz (1972: 8) states that urban areas in the circumpolar north cannot absorb all native workers; hence, unemployment and occupational dislocation of the Inuit sets in. These results impact on individuals of the north in the form of emotional depression and anxiety, which eventually lead to cases of excessive drinking, violence, and high suicide rates.

Over the past fifty-six years, as colonization and modernization of the circumpolar north increased between 1960 and 2016, modernization has certainly had some positive impact. However, social concerns are augmented as well. The most alarming has been the correlated increase in suicide rates, particularly among males aged between fifteen and twenty-five—a manifestation of many social problems and associated underlying causal factors. Thus, as southern intervention steadily increased over time, so has the suicide rate, especially for young males. Taking into account that suicide rates vary between regions of the circumpolar north, Leineweber (2000: 10) states that there was a huge increase in suicides in Greenland and northern European countries (Denmark, Finland, and Sweden). Greenland in the early 1970s had rates that were below 50 suicides per 100,000 of population; in the 1980s, the rates reached above 100 per 100,000. Between 1984 and 1989 the rates spiked between 109 and 140 per 100,000. Page 13 of Leineweber's report makes reference to the polar communities of Alaska and Canada and concludes that for the 1970s and 1980s, all indications were that there existed higher suicide rates among indigenous groups compared to the general population in Canada or the United States. The Canadian north has a high rate of suicide. The Aboriginal Healing Foundation (2007: 13–14) says that from 1999 to 2003, the suicide rate in Inuit regions across Canada averaged 135 per 100,000 in population. The report continues to say that in comparison, between 1998 and 1999, Indian Health Service estimates the rate of such deaths for the American Indian population as 19.3 per 100,000, compared to 11.2 for the general public. Problems on reserves still persist, and living conditions are often akin to living in the third world.

Suicide has reached epidemic proportions: in April, 2016, on a reserve called Attawapiskat located at the mouth of the Attawapiskat River on James Bay in Northern Ontario, populated by about two thousand and plagued by suicides for decades, eleven suicide attempts by youths were recorded, as well as twenty-eight attempts, in March alone (Canadian Press, 2016). Olson (2013: 1–5) says among the youth, suicide has become a normal response to a hopeless existence stemming from feelings of marginalization, not being able to integrate with the dominant culture, depression (mental illnesses), drug usage, sexual abuse, shame, and persecution. It appears the root of suicide, alcoholism, violence, homelessness, incarceration, and similar problems is injustices by the Canadian government of the 1960s and 1970s, which caused the eradication of culture, the loss of language, the erosion of traditional values, and the demise of the traditional family structure creating intergenerational trauma. Olson makes a special remark in his article by stating that before the nineteenth century, suicide was extremely rare in Native American communities. The culture shock that followed the penetration of European explorers, along with institutionalized racism rampant in Canadian government policies, caused a gradual increase in suicide in the twentieth century, and it continues today. The literature in this realm continuously points out that these problems are not confined to Canada's north; it is evident across all aboriginal communities around the world.

Unlike the Eskimo of yesteryear, Waltz (1972: 8) states, "So far the white world has produced few jobs for Eskimos and Indians ... Teenagers who come out of schools only drift from one menial job to another. They lean increasingly on public welfare, which gives them enough cash for escape in drink. In many cases, the young women end up in prostitution." Rhomer (1973: 189–195) concluded that governments undertake huge projects in northern areas and employ hundreds of natives, but the problem is that once projects are finished, most natives become unemployed. Such a case happened at the conclusion of the building of the Alyeska pipeline down the Mackenzie Valley. In contrast, many workers from southern areas become permanently employed in northern projects and industries; this shows signs of discrimination. Hugh Brody (1977: 336–337) provides a good discussion concerning the effects of occupational dislocation in the Canadian north. In 1977, Brody found that communities could not support all native workers, and thus in order for workers to maintain the rising standard of living in the cash economy, 15–25 percent of the labor pool was forced to find employment away from home. It was found that worker mobility causes disruption to the home communities of northern areas and disorientation of native workers. For example, Brody describes that family segregation is on the rise, family breakdowns are frequent, and crime, poverty, and loss of traditional ways of life have resulted. The problems of unemployment and occupational dislocation are but two factors among many that lead to abuse of alcohol in northern areas; Waltz (1972: 9) states, "One of the reasons people drink a lot is because there's nothing else to do … Liquor store profits should be put into recreational facilities." It has been found that in Alaska during 1981, 60 percent of deaths were accountable to alcoholism, one in every ten natives was considered alcoholic, and 31 percent of forcible rapes and 42 percent of homicides were linked to alcohol abuse (Albrecht, 1983: 601–602).

Along with the so-called advantages of northern urban settlements came the acculturation of younger generations in the circumpolar north. Two factors have contributed greatly to this process: modern schools equipped with teachers educated in major southern cities, such as Montreal, and the mass media. From the 1970s to today, many Inuit parents have been known to complain about the fact that schools in the north produced alienated, disrespectful, and disobedient children (Waltz, 1972: 9). Similarly, Muller-Wille (1975: 133) states that schools and other institutions have succeeded in wiping out the tradition and language in the youngest generations within the last two decades. In addition, graduates frequently acquire skills useless in northern contexts (Waltz, 1972:9). The factor that schools in the north are often located many miles from settlements has contributed to the degradation of culture in younger generations of the Inuit. Waltz (1972: 9) documents that hundreds of children, including those as young as first grader, are airlifted three hundred miles or more to big, modern boarding schools in Inuvik. Therefore, children are away from home for months, and parents are unable to teach their children about native lifestyles, values, and culture at impressionable ages. The last of these schools was closed in the early 1990s, however, for the children that were educated at these boarding schools and who were away from family and community for long periods of time, it contributed to deep intergenerational scars.

The other major factor that has led to the degradation of northern culture, especially among the younger generations, is the mass media, a by-product of outside economic interests. Christopher, Granzberg, and Steinbring (1983: 459–465) studied the impact of television on the people of Oxford House, a Cree village in northern Manitoba. They found that Cree response to television differed according to the age of the viewer. Older, more traditional Cree members related their viewing to their own traditions, whereas younger members were more likely to accept a standard Euro-Canadian interpretation. The results were that by 1979, Oxford House children showed changes in behavior, both general and specific, that could be attributed to the influence of television. In traditional Cree society, fighting, refusing a direct request, and raising one's voice inappropriately were considered unacceptable acts for children to do (Sindell, 1968: 88). Today, the increase in body contact and shouting that accompanies team sports among the Cree marks a notable change in the behavior of children.

Living Western and in urban settlements has not been easy for northerners. Investigating the adaptation to town life of the first indigenous generations that came into contact with southern interests sheds light on this matter. Although the younger generations of people in the northlands do not follow traditional lifestyles and culture traits of older generations to a stringent extent, they are definitely and comparatively at an advantage at the present time. Younger people who grow up under the cash economy and other southern influences have proven to be more adaptable to town life and southern language and norms than the ecologically dependent generations that had initial contact with the resource-hungry white man during the mid-1950s and throughout the 1960s and 1970s. The problems older generations had in adapting to a new lifestyle were especially evident after World War II, when prices for furs fell to a point where income from trapping alone no longer covered the cost of food and equipment needed to support the trapper's family. Thus, many untrained natives moved to expanding towns (Honigmann, 1975: 152). The jobs found in the towns required worker discipline, physical strength, skills, motivation, and knowledge. Natives had difficulties relating with supervisors (often southerners) and were largely unsuccessful in adapting with mining and industrial work environments (Honigmann, 1975: 155).

Jobs were not the only things natives found they could not cope with. Honigmann mentions that natives even had numerous problems filling out job applications, unemployment forms, and pension forms; they simply were not used to the new system introduced to them by southern cultures. Managing money is another area in which natives frequently had problems. Smith (n.d.: 32) describes how a man from Inuvik asked an anthropologist to keep a portion of his pay so that he would not be enticed to spend it all. Honigmann (1975: 158) found that families receiving a cash income had difficulties setting priorities, and many natives could not accept that they had expenses to pay before providing funds to friends and purchasing alcohol. Today, problems such as these are not as common but are still evident to some extent; more recent generations have grown accustomed to the new way of life.

Indigenous peoples who had earlier contacts with the white man had problems adapting to a new life style set by southern standards (i.e., urban living, work conditions, the cash economy, material well-being), and they also experienced the pain of losing social habits that were representative of hundreds of years of ancestry. An example of changing social habits caused by new elements in material well-being is the introduction of technology, such as nets in the Inuit settlement of Tiniteqilaq. Nooter (1975: 37–42) describes that the adoption of fishing nets put an end to a form of hunting on winter ice that knew at least some form of social organization. In earlier times arctic char were caught in a weir. Stone dams covered with water at high tide were built at the mouths of rivers. When low tide was present, the arctic char trapped between the dams were taken with harpoons or spears. Those who participated in this activity kept all the fish they caught. In order to achieve their objectives, cooperation and organization were necessary for the building and annual repair of the dams. In more contemporary times, where the dams were once located, nets are set out, checked, and emptied from a boat. Women are no longer needed to collect the fish. Further, the distance between the nets of the various hunters used to be determined by unwritten rules, but competition between hunters is now the new standard because all fishermen want to stake out their nets in the most advantageous areas. Hence the introduction of nets for catching arctic char made an existing form of social organization unnecessary. The nets also caused more family segregation as individual families could catch more with nets, and the families consumed their individual catches. A factor that reinforced family segregation has to do with house building. Nooter states that new houses built with government support in the northern settlements of the 1960s occupied one nuclear family, and therefore the daily face-to-face contact with other individuals from different families was lost. Before major influxes of southern cultures, several families lived under one roof and shared the catch.

As discussed earlier, younger indigenous generations have proven to be more adaptable to the present southern lifestyles and cultures. But as it has been pointed out, acculturation of youngsters, unemployment and dislocation, a changed social structure, and all their associated negative impacts (such as alcoholism, high death rates, and prostitution) show that living in the circumpolar north is still difficult. These types of problems are compounded when considering the fact that the vastness of northern areas and the severity of cold winters make it expensive to own transport vehicles because they require more oil and fuel, special heaters, tires, and maintenance. It has been found that these extra costs add up to 20 percent higher than in more southern areas (Wonders, 1981: 58, in Mitchell and Sewell, 1981:58). Health is another area of concern because indigenous peoples have changed their lifestyles and food consumption to resemble southerners. The effects of living more like us were shown by Haraldson (1983: 353), who states that Swedish and Finnish Lapland have similar patterns of mortality, including a significantly high prevalence of cardiovascular diseases. But Haraldson concludes that Lapps engaged in reindeer herding have a low rate of cardiovascular problems, whereas non-Lapps (i.e., woodworkers in Finland) have a higher rate, correlated with their working, living, and dietary conditions. Another problem northerners are faced with concerns the natural environment. Increased southern economic activity has attracted not only rural indigenous peoples to northern settlements but also high levels of southern workers who, in turn, create problems of waste disposal on the terrestrial and aquatic environments. The increasing economic activity taking place in all parts of the north also produces problems of toxic chemical accumulation, oil contamination, air and noise pollution, and habitat disruption for wildlife (Stirling and Calvert, 1983: 433–449). Finally, there are the issues of native self-government, land claims, and native rights. Governments have refused in most cases to give Indians rights to ancestral lands because migrants to the north must not have any problems from natives in obtaining lands and capitalizing from large-scale developments (Keith and Wright, 1978: 99–100).

The negative impacts felt by natives of the circumpolar north due to southern economic intervention must be viewed more seriously by governments. The few issues and problems discussed herein lean toward the conclusion that all northern economic development must take place at a reasonable pace—a pace that is consistent with native needs, which basically call for protection of their natural environment, their cultures and traditional way of life, a better socioeconomic status, proper education, and a decrease in social problems resulting from Western thinking and capitalistic expansion. Proper management of northern economic development can alleviate the situation, but this cannot be achieved unless fair and willful communication channels are opened between circumpolar peoples and their respective governments. There is a need to restore, improve, and maintain the life ways of the peoples we call northerners, indigenous, aboriginals, Indian, or natives. Governments hear the cry of the circumpolar peoples, but they are more concerned with power, prestige, and economic well-being for certain segments of the populations under their jurisdictions. Under these conditions, it is very likely that more negative impacts will be felt by circumpolar peoples due to outside intervention, especially when it becomes more and more economically feasible to extract resources. Realizing this, northerners will no longer sit back and watch their traditions fade away, their lands taken away, or their environment degraded. On the contrary, northerners have made some headway in the area of land claims, but there is still a long road ahead. Northern peoples have now become more like southerners: today's generation of indigenous peoples is no longer timid and appears to be putting up a fight against southern colonization. Natives now want to be involved in the planning of northern developments, and they want to know the short and long-term implications of economic development, such as impacts on their freedom, society, and the environment. These aspects are reflected in the many organizations northern natives have formed to achieve their goals. The question that remains unanswered is whether or not native organizations have enough clout to fight both public and private southern economic expansion into northern areas.

Part IV

Some Observations

Chapter 6

Burrascano: Some Observations

Introduction

I am one who likes to sometimes view our Western society and world from afar. I have lived in post-World War II Western society. I have experienced Western mentalities associated with Canadian affluence during the 1960s and 1970s, as well as the short economic recession at the beginning of the 1980s and the economic high involved with the remainder of that decade. I also experienced the long recessionary decade of the 1990s and the strong economy of the first decade of the new millennium until 2008, when the big recession hit. Now, in 2016, we are still experiencing the effects of the 2008 recession because the North American and world economy is still quite sluggish. I characterize the times as full of confusion and insecurity.

There definitely is truth to the claim that every decade has its own distinctiveness and is marked by certain trends and events. In many ways, it's good to be living in this day and age, however the new millennium (at least thus far) leaves a lot to be desired.

I felt the need to express my point of view in writing because I lack an appropriate forum. Most cannot be bothered with engaging in conversation regarding complex issues surrounding us. People have a tendency to not listen to each other very much, and they are too busy to even talk to each other. Even when conversation takes place, it is often perfunctory, and attention spans are very short. Most don't want to hear about what affects their everyday lives; there is enough activity surrounding their own individual lives, and they especially don't want to hear about more bad news. What television news gives them is enough bad news in a day.

In the last few years especially, I have spent part of my leisure time focusing on societal trends, taking the time to understand why these trends arise, and deciphering the implicit, intricate relationships involved with the fabric of these trends. The observations and conclusions herein are not ground-breaking. In our information age, enough facts and figures exist for everyone to render their own conclusions. However, most people don't take the time to examine what is going on around them that influences the society they live in and, by extension, their individual lives.

I remember going shopping at a well-known suburban Montreal shopping mall in the late 1990s. On my way out of one of the stores, my eyes caught the attention of a book sitting on a display stand that had been written by the pollster Angus Reid. The book was entitled *Shakedown: How the New Economy Is Changing Our Lives.* I purchased the book, and it lay around in my study for about two months. One day I decided to read the first chapter. The book was so good that one week later, I had finished reading it. The biggest reason I liked the book was that I was amazed to find that many conclusions Reid had reached (many from statistical evidence) were reflective of many of my observations written months earlier. I occasionally cite Reid herein.

My purposes for writing this chapter are twofold. First, I wrote this work to inform and to demonstrate that our current Western worldview can be both damaging and ameliorated. Second, I care about the issues involved and the people who have to endure the pains associated with a system they often do not comprehend; going with the flow is not always the correct way to go.

New Millennium Style Capitalism

Western society is living in grandiose times. Our urbanized industrial society has reached a pinnacle. Never before in the history of humankind has the earth witnessed such opulence and opportunity. We live in an era in which much has been accomplished, much is still possible, and many contradictions exist. We live in a time in which humanity realizes the limitations involved with the manner in which we as a civilization choose to live—environmental problems, world hunger, and many social ills can attest to this. Yes, we've travelled far, but have we progressed? The Western world now possesses sufficient information to determine the direction humanity must take to resolve problems of all sorts. Inaction or plotting the wrong course of action at this stage of our industrial era paints a bleak picture of our fate as humans living on planet earth. With the knowledge we have so far accumulated, with the studies that have been made, and with the conclusions rendered on issues such as global warming, third world poverty, social injustices, crimes of all sorts, and war, it should be easy to see where humanity should be heading to make things better and more secure.

Which world organization, which state, which educational institution, which corporation, which individual will be the one to take the leadership role and act as the unifying force in setting a proper course for our small globe and those residing on her? Isn't it time to start acting on what we already know? Is there need for more study? Aren't the conclusions sufficient grounds for implementation of some sort of unified global approach to resolving at least some of the more pressing ills of our time? Yes, certain United Nation conferences have taken place to treat certain issues, including those surrounding the environment. How effective has this been? Has our world benefited yet? Certainly someone is bound to pick an issue that has been resolved from such conferences to demonstrate their effectiveness or potential for effectiveness, I ask you, in whatever time one may be reading this analysis, have you experienced a marked improvement in world conditions? I would have to say that if some sort of very important central and global body has been designated and given sufficient powers for the sole purpose of making our world a better place, then yes. If such a body does not exist or has never existed, then the probability is that the world is in disarray. Before you make your judgment, study the world around you until you understand it enough to make a fair assessment. At this time, I can attest that based on what I know about current conditions, our world is in a sorry state but can be saved should we wish to. Waiting too long will take us to the point of no return. If we're not careful now, I foresee a world in much greater shambles. In your time of reading these sentiments, should the world be in a fabulous circumstance, I congratulate all parties concerned; you have done well and continue to take the actions necessary to preserve or better what you have accomplished. My hope is that it is this last statement that stands—otherwise, someone somewhere out there has a lot of work to do.

Fortunately, the world of academia influences the minds of individuals who will someday contribute to bettering society. These graduates leave academia with much enthusiasm, knowledge, goodwill, and intentions. They eventually enter the so-called real world and find they've travelled back in time because for one reason or another, the real world isn't as nice, fair, or rational as it should be. Still, even under these circumstances, they can either go astray and follow everybody else, or take on the obligation to contribute to furthering the cause of making the world a better place by living in a way that perpetuates good for all. The beauty in this is that one can choose to contribute in the ways one finds fit. You see, my way of doing it for the time being is to inform. Your way may be to help those in need, or to teach, or to make your company a fairer place to work in, or make corporate production more environmentally safe. One may even want to simply be nice to people and bring out good feelings that in their own way translate into actions for the good. It is up to these graduates to ameliorate world conditions and each new graduating class lays a foundation to a better world.

The reality is that the notions absorbed in academia are much more pristine than that which is practiced in the "real world." Under the current capitalist society, morals, values, and beliefs are challenged, and the profit motive is key. People work like machines, think for themselves, and compete against each other. Family life becomes secondary to career in many instances, and discrimination is based on gender, age, looks and color, ethnicity, scholarliness, and economic class. Our young are neglected, our aged are put aside, our spiritual side is compromised or put on hold, there exists no uniform consensus on the manner in which we should lead our lives, we don't have time for ourselves or others, we create crimes against each other, world economies are suffering, wars loom somewhere in the world, civil unrest is present elsewhere, hunger and poverty persist in many countries, and the natural world faces disaster. It is more apparent that our hope for a better world must lie in academia, where the concerns for humanity are analyzed and questioned in a more objective and genuinely concerned fashion, and in a tone that speaks in the best interest of humankind rather than in the best interest of some political party, faction, lobby group, nation, corporation, or individual. Change for the better must come from the individual because governments have failed to set a proper course for humanity.

The root of the problem is capitalism and its inherent economy and profit motive. Much is put aside to serve economic growth, and much is sacrificed by individuals to accumulate wealth. Humanity's ultimate sacrifice has been the slow disintegration of global collective piece of mind, the natural environment, and perhaps the extinction of the human race. How serious is the question of the extinction of the human race? I truly don't want to be alarmist, however some view this question in the following manner. Edwards (2010) explains that Frank Fenner, an eminent Australian scientist, emeritus professor of microbiology at the Australian National University in Canberra, author and co-author of 22 books and 290 scientific papers and book chapters, and contributor to the eradication of smallpox, believes that humans will be extinct in one hundred years. Fenner believes the situation is irreversible because the anthropogenic impact on earth during the industrial era (unofficially known as the Anthropocene period) is similar to effects of ice ages or comet impacts. Fenner believes that climate change is only at the beginning stages but is likely to be the culprit of our extinction. He also believes that an explosion in world population will cause us to overuse natural resources, and thus animals and humans will not be able to survive.

Do we listen to our politicians, who often have hidden agendas governed by polls and votes, who basically are actors putting on a show to influence us, and who have taken us in the wrong direction for decades and have been out of touch with what people really need? Or do we listen to some person coming out of school and genuinely wanting the world to be a better place? Do we look up to those that are wealthy, have great looks, or portray the traits that capitalism tells us to value, or are we sophisticated enough to make a more objective decision and listen to ourselves? In my judgment, other people's wealth does not make them more right or better than you or me. If one's own objective is to be wealthy, that person may be interested in listening to or copying those who portray the traits of successful capitalists, but not everyone's objective in life is the attainment of significant wealth, and those individuals have the right to go about their lives to obtain satisfaction in other ways suitable to them. After all, the definition of success for a person may not be the same as that of another. In our Western culture, success is often defined as possessing material wealth and the associated social status and privileges. To someone else, being successful may mean something else. For example, success can also be defined by having good health, a steady employment, a healthy family life, a good sense of self, peace of mind, appreciation of living things, and a simpler approach to life. It all depends on what we put our values on.

Capitalism insinuates the struggle to succeed and stay at the top. For many, they may not feel that life must always be an upward struggle all the time—or at all. The capitalist economy demands this struggle. How high do you want to go? If one chooses not to reach the top, is that necessarily bad? According to Western society, it is, because this is nonperpetual anticapitalist behavior and is often unfairly labeled as a sign of laziness, lack of ability, lack of intelligence, and whatever label one wants to attach. Is this better thinking? We must not judge people who do not necessarily want to be part of the capitalist mold characterized by accumulation of wealth, material well-being, and status because they may be just as happy or happier than the person with the struggle for success as defined under capitalism. In fact, those who don't feel the need for incredible success or its associated struggle may be contributing to society and the economy in other ways, such as by creating balancing forces with capitalism. For instance, capitalist behavior is often aggressive compared to those having a more docile approach to things, and it often replaces spirituality with material, compared to those who have the tendency to spread spirituality and faith. Capitalists often do little to help the natural world, compared to the existence of citizens concerned for the environment. Capitalists don't have enough time to think of others, compared to those who perform community volunteer work. Although this vague balance exists, capitalist forces are by far stronger in our society and in most instances negate neutralizing efforts both domestically and internationally.

One of the biggest ills of the capitalist economy is that it gets people caught up in a vortex, and people do get carried away. Yes, there are the very few success stories, but how many try just as hard or harder but can't complete the struggle to attain significant wealth or success as defined under capitalism and by our culture? We've heard about those committing suicide because they've lost fortunes. We've heard of young and old persons who have gone on shooting rampages, killing and injuring people of all ages because they gave in to the various types of pressures stemming from capitalism and often inherent pressures demanded by our perfectionist culture. We've heard of those addicted to gambling. We've heard of countless examples of those working very hard to attain substantial wealth, but in the process they've lost their health, serenity, or families. Our capitalist system offers many advantages, but these few examples represent some of the negative results experienced by people living in the capitalist economy. Temptation, the drive to succeed, and the exorbitant pressure put upon us by capitalism at crucial times often cause poor judgment calls and blur our vision of priorities, of right and wrong, and of our treatment of others (and by extension the natural world). When one's major preoccupation in life becomes money, individuals prioritize their lives in a manner that is unbalanced. One lives to make money, but all else becomes secondary or tertiary, such as the nuclear family, caring for others, having meaningful conversation or relationships, or taking time to find one's self or find peace within the natural world. I have concluded that for as long as it exists, we must let capitalism serve us—but we should not serve it! We must compromise with it and reach a balance in which we use it to our advantage without destroying ourselves.

Alas, the truth is that our society is in the process of disintegration. Our extremely short era of industrialism will come to an end in correlation with the decline of fossil fuels. Perhaps in the next era, referred to as the solar age, humanity's morals, values, and beliefs will have evolved to a more fine-tuned level in which the basis for existence is not accumulation of wealth or power, but the improvement of human beings to a degree that allows them to be in harmony with all global cultures and the natural world. The very short industrial era will probably be seen as part of a primitive Western civilization one day, compared to our current belief that we are so supreme and advanced. The question that remains is whether or not our civilization will have the time to complete the transition to the new solar age in light of current and still hidden environmental problems.

It is clear that capitalism is for wealth accumulation by states, corporations, and private citizens, and there is absolutely nothing wrong with that concept. In fact, I do not consider myself to be anticapitalist; I am a contributor and participant in the capitalist system, and I believe that Canada is a great nation. My concern is with the inherent shortfalls of our system, and I want to bring attention to issues that merit readjustment and solutions. I am not so naive as to claim that I can survive without it presently, but the system is not as perfect as some profess. My hope is that these observations can somehow lead us toward changing our thinking about how we should approach complex problems. The fact is that capitalism and industrialism are human-made and are not natural. I would go as far as to say that just as religion has sometimes been used in certain cultures to oppress and make politically subservient the populations of numerous countries around the world, we in the Western world have chosen to replace religion with capitalism and nationalism, and we have been brainwashed by capitalism and its supporters to serve its goals of wealth accumulation and power. Even many proverbs support capitalism, such as "It takes money to make money," or "Money makes the world go round," or "Money talks," or "Survival of the fittest," or "Where would we be without progress?" Then there's the notorious saying "To each his own," or the proverb that says something to the effect of, "Don't bite the hand that feeds you." What about the nationalistic saying "Having the American (or

Canadian) dream"? Capitalism demands human behavior, habits, response, action, and tendencies that are not natural or humanly. In many ways, you are really not the problem; capitalism demands that you proceed in certain ways, or else you don't succeed.

Closely associated with capitalism is technology. Human physiology was not intended to go to or reside on the moon or in space, but technology has allowed this to happen. We've gone out of our way to culturally adapt to the demands of capitalism rather than the demands of nature and spirituality. Many recent wars have been the result of capitalism. I consider the first American landing on the moon as war and an extension of the Cold War arms race because the reason behind it was to demonstrate to the world American (and I would include allied) world power and supremacy, wealth and technological know-how, and ultimately the superiority of the capitalist system over all other forms of social, political, and economic systems around the globe, especially that of the Soviet Union. I ask you, was the Gulf War (Desert Storm) of the early 1990s intended to free the citizens of Kuwait from Iraqi occupation, or was it intended to secure oil reserves for Western capitalist consumption—or some other reason? As Desert Fox of 1998 demonstrated, I am afraid I do not doubt that someday, somehow, and somewhere the Western world will again exercise its ego militarily, and we may not be as lucky as we were at the end of the Cold War, especially in light of some nations who are in possession of nuclear and chemical weaponry to protect themselves from

Western colonization. I leave it to your imagination to figure out why international spying and terrorism exists. The Western ego is still very active as we boast of our economic and technological well-being without taking into account the perils surrounding our own nations, such as environmental and social problems. As a note, I need to include that a lot of our civilian technological know-how and improvement in technology stems from war, because inventions and improvements in existing technology during past major wars and the Cold War were required to provide the upper hand against enemy nations.

As Westerners, we cannot travel this world with the ethnocentric conviction that our way of living is the correct or only way of living. Other cultures are also entitled to live as they please. Did you ever think that international problems exist because many cultures were simply not left alone by industrializing imperialist nations? Can you imagine certain world countries highly based on religion wanting to become industrialized in the first place? We impose ourselves, and some don't like it and are forced to rebel against us because they don't want to conform to the industrialization and colonization from the Western world—so we then bomb them from the air! They become the bad guys, and we portray ourselves as the good guys. Remember, not so long ago the Russians were seen as the bad guys! Remember the cowboys and Indians television shows and movies? Indians were virtually always portrayed as the bad guys! Remember, environmentalists have been seen as the bad guys! Anyone who resists or does not conform to the capitalist agenda becomes an enemy. Thus, we have broken rule number one: we as Westerners have sometimes not respected our fellow coinhabitants of this earth. Do you expect other nations of this world to trust and respect us? It comes down to the same thing between individuals: if I don't use respect with people in front of me, can I expect them to respect me back? They may tolerate it at that very moment, but I shouldn't expect their trust, good faith, or respect any time after that. No one is stupid, and the problems start!

Why do we put so much faith in a system that is evidently in decline, soiling the natural world, and often treats its own people and those of other nations unequally and unfairly? Let me put it to you this way: the capitalist system provides a good living for some people. If one can stay above the poverty line or do even better, the likelihood of public complaint or protest is diminished. When economic problems set in and enough people are suffering, the capitalist system falters and can collapse. Capitalism works because many people living in the system are not familiar with its intricate workings and impacts, and this causes people to be passive toward the system. Second, Western populations have been brainwashed to the greatest extent by politicians, some of the best salespeople who have ever existed, to believe that our system is the greatest and most viable there is. It is easy to convince the populations under capitalist jurisdiction and less developed nations of this because capitalism has given North Americans and Western Europeans a very comfortable lifestyle and standard of living, not to mention many civil liberties. Many people, including myself, are very thankful for this. I am often awed by what our Western civilization has accomplished and the opportunities the system still offers. My concern, however, is at whose expense, and at what expense? Does it make sense to live in the manner in which we do and yet disrupt the delicate environmental balances that exist in nature or hurt each other as humans? Is there another less environmentally destructive form of capitalism? Is there a more equitable side to capitalism internationally? Is there a more human connotation involved with this system based on cold, hard cash?

Based on these questions alone, is current capitalism a threat to itself? Think about the effectiveness of our economic system during times of depression such as the 1930s or recessions felt in the early 1980s and most of the 1990s, as well as the sluggish beginning of the second decade of the new millennium. Think of the racial barriers that exist, think of the shrinking middle class and poverty stricken or homeless in our society. Think of a degrading environment that cannot sustain the opulence offered by such a system. Is the capitalist system in its present state self-defeating?

Our present economy demands efficiency, and we are employing all kinds of efficient reasoning, persons, and technologies in our corporations. There is no room for less efficient persons or technology.

What happens when our economy reaches great efficiency? We are already witnessing that technology has eliminated vast numbers of jobs, and the law of survival of the fittest has put thousands in unemployment or underemployment. Could Karl Marx's prediction become true? Will the capitalist system become overefficient in increasing both production and consumption, and will it fall? On the production side, we can state that when production becomes overefficient with the application of technology, there are not enough people working to earn wages and salaries to consume and drive the mechanism of supply and demand.

My constitution for expressing these observations on paper is intended for the preservation and amelioration of our standard of living. My point is that there must exist other ways of assuring a good standard of living in a manner that doesn't compromise nature and the human experience and is accessible to all, both domestically and internationally. No matter how wonderful technology is perceived and is functional (especially in medicine), can we meet a point of safe equilibrium with it? Not all problems inherent to capitalism can be solved with technical know-how—we must give it a more human face. I have reached the conclusion that if any change for the better is to arise, our collective thoughts, meanings, attitudes, morals, values, and beliefs must be altered to a point that is not manly aggressive but more docile, such as the feminine side of caring. I am tempted to ask you, will the points of view presented herein put a new twist on things for you to the meaning of the phrase we commonly hear, "Without progress we have nothing"? Do we necessarily want to spread capitalism in its present form around the world?

When our capitalist system falters, especially when there is a lack of jobs domestically, we begin to understand the limitations involved. Built-in economic buffers and other forms of government intervention keep the system from falling. This is why Western governments choose to invest public funds in programs that maintain and stimulate economic growth and job creation. I call this "buying time." In Canada, much more money is poured into, say, regional economic development than programs geared toward the protection of the environment. It comes down to political priorities, and keeping the economy on its feet is more important for governments than other important social issues. This is called planned economic development, and it is designed to kick-start the economy to create jobs and boost consumer confidence, spending, and investment. We don't have to look far into history to understand how important a role government has played in economic development. Consider what the United States did for post–World War II economically ravaged Europe with implementation of the Marshall Plan until 1951. Consider what was done in the United States to surpass the hurdle of the Great Depression. Consider what has been done in Canada during recent prolonged recessions. How many social programs have been eliminated, modified, or rebuilt because they became a frowned-upon expense for government in comparison to reducing the heavy burden of national debt or directing public monies to sectors of activity and regions that create economic spin-offs of a perpetual type? Even the national pension fund, the arts, and education are threatened! Although all levels of government have demonstrated more concern for the natural environment (due in part to public pressure), they have generally not allocated tons of money to environmental causes, specific groups, or individuals concerned with nature because should these groups gain sufficient funding, it would give them more strength and power to deflate the efforts made by government in creating economic growth.

Employment and the Economy

During the North American economic recession of the 1990s and the sluggish economic periods since, we experienced the extent to which government and the economy affects society and culture. One can examine the effects of government decisions to redirect funds into policies and programs that stimulate the economy and decrease funding to programs of a social type such as health care, employment insurance, and education. Private enterprise responded to recession in much the same manner as government: by downsizing and redirecting financial resources to activities that would assure the viability of companies. The result has been, in my view, a dramatic shift in the way North American society perceives the world and their place in it. At one time, religion and spirituality alone helped drive the economies of the world by encouraging the union of young adults through the institution of marriage. Once married, couples were encouraged to have children. Although spirituality, marriage, and childbirth can be wonderful experiences, the creation of a single household also implied demands on the economy to supply such things as food, housing, furniture, clothing, transportation, education, and entertainment. All this demand creates employment, and employment creates disposable income, which continues to fuel the economy.

I would say that prior to World War II until the early 1970s OPEC oil crises, a period of unprecedented sustained economic growth in both developed and developing countries, spirituality, and its support of the building of the nuclear family worked well for Western economies. One vital point contributed to this aside from political stability: an understanding in our culture that respect was important for good relations between people; this extended into the workplace. The nuclear family as an institution was perceived as important in society. The result was that employers were more apt to being more responsible toward employees, especially if they were married and had a household to financially support. This contributed to a sense of direction for people, confidence, and most important stability for employees (often men) who were considered the heads of nuclear families during that era. Stability at work meant disposable income for families, which drove the Western economy to massive development. This was particularly evident during the post-war period of the 1950s and 1960s. In the 1970s it became fashionable (or a necessity) for women to seek employment, and this further contributed to the expansion of the Western economy because it meant more disposable income for families. The beginning of the 1980s was recessionary, but the decade proceeded at full momentum for much of its duration. In general, from the 1990s until the present day, Western economies have moved along and have experienced ups and downs.

Midway into the second decade of the new millennium, we find the Western economy and the world economy sluggish. For many reasons, our society finds that even with two-income households, annual familial revenue simply isn't enough to fulfill the exuberant needs and insatiable wants of a highly materialistic society, and high unemployment doesn't help the situation. During the 1980s and 1990s, we went from the "me" generation to the selfish generation, and in 2016 it doesn't appear we've become less selfish. The manner in which government and private enterprise responded to counteract the ills of sluggish economies brought about the worse in us as a society and a shift in the manner North Americans choose to live. This choice is going in a direction that doesn't perpetuate capitalism. The capitalist system already appears to be in shambles, and people are beginning to question it. This is highly evident when one considers the sarcasm and distrust that has set in about politicians. In their own way, people appear to have acknowledged that the system has many flaws and often does not suit their needs. They feel disillusioned. Angus Reid (1997: 257, 273) writes, "The Canadian public is frustrated, angry, and restless, and rightfully so. Canadians have little faith in the contradictory signals they are receiving from politicians." He also adds, "Canadian voters are now less likely to retain allegiance to any single party and more likely to call themselves independents."

Western society may still perceive itself as a community and society sharing a common culture, but we certainly don't act like it. Today, we are more individualistic than in past decades, and we feel increasing pressure to do something extraordinary, like be rich and famous, in order to be viewed as standing apart from the rest. After all, isn't this what the capitalist economy wants us to do? Even government has become more selfish through privatization of certain Crown activities, cutbacks of many social programs and services, and implementation of hidden taxes and user fees. Government has decreased its responsibilities toward citizens, leaving it to the private sector to pick up the slack, however the private sector has failed in picking up that slack. Just as government has become more selfish, so has private enterprise. No longer do private businesses feel a certain onus of responsibility toward its employees, the heads of nuclear families. The employment security these people need to contribute to the economy by purchasing a new home, having one or more children, or putting enough money aside for retirement simply isn't there! People have been laid off in large numbers during recent economic recessions due to lack of work, and many lose their jobs because they can't meet preestablished monetary quotas in sales. Others are let go because they don't fit the corporate mold, or because they stand up for their dignity and rights. Then there are those who cannot find employment because they have just finished school and do not possess sufficient experience or lack aggressive business behavior. In addition, many hardworking and loyal folks are paid low wages and salaries, and gender still plays a role because female employees are often paid lower than men. Younger people living at home with their parents are often discriminated against with low pay because of their age and marital status. There still exists a general negative perception of blacks and minorities in the workplace. Employers and human resource personnel still ask questions to potential employees that are illegal, and this often presents obstacles to being hired.

Already the workplace is an uneven playing field in which there exists a boss and a subordinate. This social organization in the workplace has been abused. Employees are often not treated fairly due to limited financial resources of the company, poor management and supervision, lack of benefits, lack of training, favoritism, and discrimination. Thus, in this heightened period of Western economic problems, the workplace is a good indicator of our society's status: tough times can bring out the worse in us. If employers feel no loyalty toward their employees, are employees going to be loyal to their employers? Do productivity and creativity excel in the workplace under these circumstances? Probably not—hence, the economy cannot move forward as strongly as we would want. These are some of the reasons why people often no longer stay in one job for long periods of time. This creates instability, and countless many cannot afford to make plans that involve money, such as getting married, purchasing a new home or a new car, or opening a business. This is behavior that is already modifying the face of capitalism because it does not perpetuate it; the economic spin-off effects involved with forward and backward linkages are diminished. Furthermore, many young people choose to get married at a later stage of life—or not get married at all. Many who are married choose to have fewer children than in previous decades or have no children. This is why statistics have shown that the birth rate in Western industrial nations is very low. The number one reason for divorce is household money problems, which has given rise to single-parent families, many of which live below the poverty line and don't contribute to the economy.

I ask you, can the economy prosper when people are no longer following a lifestyle that perpetuates capitalism? The lack of a strong economy translates into lack of funding needed to resolve major issues such as those regarding the environment, health care, poverty, and third world malnutrition. One way or the other, in the government or the private sector of Western economies, there now exists an important lack of economic and cultural support structure for the family, which inhibits the goal of creating and maintaining the nuclear family. This has arisen because the goal is no longer spiritual (as in the case of building families), but is individualistic and selfish (as in attaining personal and corporate profit). Statistics show that nuclear families that stay together have a better chance to prosper financially than if one acts individualistically; however, the trend appears to show that marriage is on the way out unless the cultural economy favors it.

Acknowledging the above sentiments, I feel compelled to present you with a radical notion. Labor unions are often perceived as bad, and they are greatly despised by many sectors of the economy. No matter what judgment one makes of them, no matter what label one wants to attach to them, no matter whether one feels they shouldn't exist—hypothetically, wouldn't unions be good for industrial economies in general, including the individuals within them? Governments are already relying on the private sector too much to keep their economies going. Governments cannot expect private enterprises to plan the direction of an economy because they do not plan for the benefit of all; they plan for the benefit of their own organizations. Governments must take the leadership role. Private enterprise is given too much freedom to take advantage of employees. It is basic, private enterprise, and the economy will benefit greatly if and when employees are happy because they will then perform better. Governments may have rules and regulations in place designed to protect employees, but they are not effective because they are largely not enforced. Above all, the government must step in and curb the sometimes questionable actions of the private sector toward employees. If the government fails to do so, shouldn't our society rely on some sort of organization that represents the best interest of employees? Protecting the rights of employees will provide the stability needed to make the economy significantly stronger.

In certain countries of Europe, already there exist more stringent policies for the protection of jobs. From the outset, isn't it unfair that some are protected by unions or have handsome benefit programs, and others have neither of these luxuries? Why should someone performing the same tasks in the public service be paid higher or lower than someone in the private sector? Is it fair that some folks can retire from their work and receive an additional pension from a company that was responsible enough to implement such a policy, but others who have worked just as long and hard are not entitled? Why is training not an important part of employment today? Is the sink-or-swim attitude fair? Are performance appraisals doing what they were intended to do? Why are laws not changed to make it more difficult to dismiss someone? In Canada, I'm afraid that the federal government does not do enough to give stability to employees. In the government's mind, it is not good for the economy when employees have too much protection—but that doesn't make business sense.

Consider these examples. A supervisor can be entitled to a handsome benefits package, but employment laws don't require a company to provide the same benefits to his subordinates. A boss is allowed to tell you at the point of hiring that you will be paid $45,000, and two or more weeks later he can reduce your pay for whatever reason he sees fit. The employment laws you are told are there to protect you lean more toward protecting business for the benefit of the wider economy. This is why many who are employed are paid very little; Angus Reid (1997: 279) calls it being on "welfare with dignity." This is the main cause of a shrinking middle class, and it is the reason why many can easily fall into poverty. In most instances, it isn't laziness, lack of intelligence or motivation, or lack of experience or education, that doesn't allow people to work; it is the economic health of the times and the disorganized and disoriented corporate and governmental executives that choose to make shortsighted decisions for short-term benefits. This sometimes includes poor treatment of employees. We need planned economic growth from a central body or a more centralized federal government. Governments must stop panicking in front of the demands of the private sector and globalization. In my judgment, government response must be one that is driven by what is good for the people and not solely for what is good for the economy or to gain votes in the next election. Many may argue that what is good for the economy is good for the people, but we are experiencing firsthand that this is not always true because current policies are making it much easier for individuals and families to sink into poverty. Consider the upsurge of people now reliant on food banks! Does this contribute to capitalism? In addition, what is currently good for industrial economies is not good for the natural environment, because without a healthy, natural environment to sustain industrial economies, there would not be an economy. Therefore, does a degraded natural environment contribute to capitalism?

We practically spend more time at work than we do at home during weekdays. We've been told work is supposed to be an enriching experience, but is it? Maybe it was at one time in our past. The workplace today is in a sad state and is full of unwritten rules and contracts. Often we are placed in an environment of falsehoods. Imagine what we do simply to keep our jobs! Many must plead poor because if they're well-off, they don't deserve the job. Many are restricted in saying what they feel, especially because they cannot go against the corporation's philosophy. People's good qualities are hindered in the wrong work environment; if you are good, others need to compete with you to prove they are better. What about getting the feeling that you are taken advantage of because you are in financial need or have a mortgage to pay and a family to support? How about the many times companies expect people to work overtime for free? What about the stress you have to endure? What about falling victim to on-the-job discrimination or sexual harassment and unwarranted put-downs?

How about being in a dead-end job, putting up with poor management and a lack of motivational stimulus? What about accepting the hidden agendas of management? In any manner one chooses to view all this, work is set up in a way that aims at getting the most out of you at least cost to the entity hiring you for the benefit of the company you're working for, and by extension the benefit of the capitalist economy and system. You are a money-making machine! Your family unit is like a business because a revenue is made, and then it is disposed of for many purposes in the wider economy.

The Rich Get Richer, and the Poor Get Poorer

I want to touch base on the issue of the rich getting richer and the poor getting poorer. It is well understood why the gap between rich and poor nations exists. We must also realize that the gap between rich and poor exists even within nations of the so-called advanced world. At its most fundamental level, the distinction between rich and poor can be considered relative because one may still be rich even if he or she does not possess monetary wealth. I conclude that those coming from stronger economic stratums are more likely to succeed in school and excel in the workplace because they have the financial strength to stimulate their motivation and overcome rough times, even when they are not making much money. They have what I would call a more solid personal infrastructure. This does not mean that someone originating from a background with less wealth cannot do well monetarily, however I leave it to your imagination to decipher what kind of struggle is involved for the majority in attaining substantial wealth, including emotional wealth. Who do you think can withstand one or more poor business investments? If one invested a great deal of money in a project and it didn't work, that person would be at a loss even if she was strong in character. Someone with ample financial resources would lose little or nothing, except her ego would be bruised temporarily, and she could later say, "Let's move on to another project." Yes, the opportunities exist for all, but it will probably be the wealthier who can withstand the vicissitudes of the struggle involved.

This is partly why the rich get richer and the poor get poorer. It doesn't mean that the rich guy is smarter than you, more motivated than you, better looking than you, or better educated than you—it's simply that the capitalist system favors his financial resources. The very small percentage of wealthy people have their share of problems too, but they are more likely to be emotionally healthy and secure for the next challenge, compared to those caught up in the vortex of the capitalist struggle in order to make enough money to survive from week to week or to become financially independent. It is not a level playing field, and this is partly why economic stratification exists. In the workplace, often the attitude one portrays at a job interview or after being hired determines whether or not one will be hired and be allowed to continue to work. Attitude in the workplace today is often just as important, or more important, as qualifications because employers seek positive people. What is often subconsciously looked for is anyone who is wealthy or demonstrates the traits or potential of the wealthy. Employers often believe that this is the kind of thinking that creates wealth for their companies in our present Western economies. It is believed that extreme positivism is good for business; the "rah, rah, rah" attitude means you're a winner, a go-getter.

Tell me, is it humanly possible for one to lead his life at 150 kilometers per hour and be extremely positive all the time? Maybe during work hours, one can keep a fast pace for a limited amount of time, but something will give if it's for a chronic amount of time. What gives out can be one's health, marriage, family life, or other life matters. In any case, I do have to say that as in many other areas of life (including health), those coming from wealthier backgrounds stand to do better in the positivism department because they have a lot to be positive about, and this is transferred into the workplace and can give them an edge over other coworkers regarding job advancement. Positive people are seen as more efficient, and this is what the upper echelons of the corporate world seek today to improve profit margins, leaving behind the vast pool of talent who didn't or couldn't live up to expectations. This is another scenario representing the fact that the rich get richer and the poor get poorer. It is the same as comparing it to the fashion modeling industry, which selects those men and women considered beautiful enough to model showcase clothing on catwalks and in fashion magazines over those who are less marketable.

Education

I want to elaborate a little on education. The education system as a whole is an integral engine in capitalist societies. I am afraid that I foresee the misuse of this institution, especially at the university level, because such institutions should be highly independent to convey an unbiased and pristine education to students. University especially is the place where one can grasp an appreciation of the pristine nature of life, nature, and the human experience. Capitalism, however, has spread its tentacles even in this most sacred of institutions. Universities have increasingly begun to produce research and provide results on matters that perpetuate capitalism in its present form, and many programs are increasingly slanted toward integration with private industry to develop talent oriented for those industries. We have reached a point where one goes to school for the sole purpose of having a better chance to find employment rather than for contributing to a better world. Decide for yourself whether or not today's ethics reach the level where, say, a student studying law goes to law school with the righteous frame of mind to first serve those in need. Or is it to graduate and have the prestigious title, social status, and potential high income associated with the profession? I feel sorry for today's students in any field of study because they have a hard time finding jobs once they graduate, and thus the current economic system forces them to think for themselves first, rather than others. It is a correct and logical choice they make, but is it a healthy one for the rest of society and the wider world?

In my view, there is elevated pressure on universities to work more closely with industry and to produce graduates that meet the labor demands of the high-tech industry. Even lower level studies put emphasis on and encourage students to orient themselves toward mathematics and hard sciences. I believe that both hard and soft sciences belong under the umbrella of university, but the side of university I have always preferred is the one dealing with humans, because university was created for the advancement of humanity. Certainly technology plays a role in the progress of capitalism, and with reservation I admit our own well-being, but it doesn't always contribute to putting human interests in the forefront. Imagine this: technology exists to kill people in war, and technology exists in agricultural production, but countless starve to death around the world every day. Chemical technology exists for many purposes, but is your drinking water really safe? All kinds of technology exist, but who is caring for the sick? Who is caring for the homeless? Who is caring about acid rain? Who is becoming a priest to disseminate spirituality? In my opinion, there is a higher probability that those with a background in the soft sciences are more likely to contribute directly to the best interests of humans on a one-to-one basis. I am referring to occupations such as nursing, social work, law, teaching, psychology, child care, community affairs and journalism, theology, and the fine arts.

In my opening, I alluded to the fact that if human and environmental conditions are to ameliorate significantly, university graduates are the ones that must contribute to this endeavor from one graduating class to the next. However, with the long arm of capitalism, is this at all possible today? Consider that students from the hard sciences are usually paid higher than those with a background in soft sciences, at least right after graduation. This is a result of the fact that capitalism puts so much emphasis on technology that associated industries can afford to pay higher salaries. Isn't capitalism at work here? Hard science is perceived as the one that is a direct contributor to capitalism, and this is why it is often more valued in the workplace. The perception is graduates from the hard sciences generally make more money than others graduating from the soft sciences. Does that make them more intelligent or useful, or is capitalism saying those who contribute more to its advancement should be paid higher? Teachers are often paid less than many employees they helped graduate! This has happened because teaching is seen more like a soft science.

I begin to appreciate a culture that isn't all about money or the law of supply and demand. In some aspects, Japan is more advanced than us.

Their economic culture, although capitalist, pays its teachers higher than our own. Isn't this right? Teachers shape the minds of the next generation! A company will not easily lay off workers for the sole reason of making higher profit; rather, they see it as bad to lay off employees, because laid-off workers do not contribute to the economy in the first place. Now, I am not saying that all Japan does is better than us, but looking at other economic cultures sheds light on where we in the Western world stand. Western capitalism cannot continue to focus on business at the expense of everything else.

The Canadian Household

Let's touch base with the Canadian experience. In the 1970s and 1980s, millions wondered about how the world would be in the 2000s. Well, the 2000s arrived. Most were in awe in the sense that the new millennium would present us a promising world; it was viewed as a new time and portrayed in the most positive of ways. When I was in my early teens, I can recall one evening sitting at the kitchen table and joking around with my mother and younger brother Filippo about all sorts of things. A special moment came that evening when my mother looked forward in time and jovially said what a special time it would be. Today, I can say that it is an exciting time for me because I am one of the lucky who can someday say, "I have lived in two centuries, the 1900s and 2000s." It is a special period because the world has still not set a proper course, much is still possible, and a cloud of problems still lurks over us. It is a time in which global societies realize it is time for change in many of our ways, and questions exist as to whether or not these changes will occur so that thousands of future generations can call earth their home.

Can we really say that the new millennium has taken us toward better living? In the last fifty years, Canadian society has gone through major changes, and not all of it has been for the better. Angus Reid (1997: 221) states, "Moral arguments don't carry much weight in the 1990's. Warnings about excessive preoccupation with building a competitive rather than humane society tend to be dismissed as outdated knee-jerk liberalism." This is most evident in the workplace. Changes in the workplace regarding cutbacks in jobs, more efficient technology, and employee expendability are causing changes in the household. According to Reid (1997: 222–250):

> … loss of jobs and lower wages and benefits and poor household finances are causing decreases in household expenditures as consumption of personal goods and services declined between 1989 and 1995. The result has been that consumers now want a good or service if it saves time, they prefer function over fashion, and they will keep what they have for longer periods of time.

This does not perpetuate capitalism, and in fact, signs are already appearing in Canadian society that indicate our morals, values, and beliefs are changing in a way that will further erode the societal behavior that sustains capitalism as we know it. Proof is found in the following summary of Reid (1997: 219–250):

> The likelihood is that over the next few decades, there will be more emphasis placed on emotional growth rather than the post-war preoccupation with material well-being. Canadian households are demonstrating renewed interest in stronger family ties and the divorce rate has declined as personal and family values are making a big comeback. Canadians are spending more time in the security of their own homes and there seems to be renewed interest in spirituality.

This is an inadvertent and nonloquacious rebellion against capitalism. People appear to be resigned to the fact that in order to live better lives, they must be willing to have less so that they can control events around them, such as a loss of employment. Today, having less and being thrifty means having some sort of stability because financial resources of the household are limited and the potential to climb into higher income brackets is more restricted. It is a new lifestyle for many—the beginning of a new economic class! Stretching household financial resources means taking risks and accepting from the outset that fears of personal losses are plausible; one can put oneself in a situation where one may lose one's home, car, vacations, and nuclear family. How long are individuals willing to live under these conditions? The observations made by Reid are enlightening and empowering in the sense that society is showing trends that are more down to earth, and less consumption is better for the environment. However, have these trends arisen because we have improved as Westerners, or are they merely a response to struggling national economies and horrible household finances? What will happen to these confirmed trends should Western economies prosper as they once did?

Our Young

I feel the need to express my point of view regarding the young living in the Western world. Just as environmental issues have been tossed aside during our economic problems, our young have been neglected. Sure, some political party in power may step forward from time to time and boast about the implementation of job creation programs for the youth, but this is what I consider a Band-Aid measure, a temporary solution to a problem that has more profound and interconnected reasons behind it. Our young are put out to pasture at a time in their lives when they can be influenced in good ways. This is the time in the life cycle of a human being that requires nurturing, but instead our children are taught to value material things, be aggressive, expect instant gratification, and strive for individualism rather than collectivism. These are traits passed on to them from their parents, extended family, friends, school, the media, and stemming from capitalism itself. What happened to older people's approach to the young?

We now have latchkey kids, with children focusing their attention on technology and many things of a nonspiritual nature. Kids are not given sufficient attention and love, and they are educated in schools to be self-reliant and not community oriented. We have kids who are influenced to become disrespectful and who are victims of broken families.

Until recently, our young were viewed as very valuable, the next contributors to a better society. Now they are seen as a burden. What happened to the attitude that any child could be the next president or prime minister? Children, teenagers, and young adults are belittled rather than encouraged to do good. Our young are often so disillusioned that they drop out of school prematurely and get into many different kinds of problems. Even for those who obtain higher education, nobody believes in them enough to offer employment, and the young adults become disillusioned, frustrated, and unproductive. Once young people (including those who graduate from higher level studies) find employment, they are often forced to go into the workplace with little or no training, and they must accept low-ranking, poorly paid positions. Today we speak of the existence of Generation X and Generation Y. These are the products of our society. Many in Generations X and Y lack direction because they don't have good role models and societal support.

It will be interesting to see how the next generation, known as Generation Z (born between 1995 and 2012), integrates in Western society. These are predominantly the children of the Generation X cohort, and their coming of age is between 2013 and 2020. In 2004, this group was aged between zero and nine. Jim Edwards (2015) says this generation represents 69 million persons or 22 percent of the US population. The main characteristic of this group is that it is the first to be born with the Internet, and they have had easy access from a very young age to the Internet and social media. Marketing firm Frank N. Magid & Associates (2012) says that the important economic recession of 2008 has caused Generation Z to be independent and entrepreneurial after experiencing their parents' and siblings' struggle in the workforce and the related financial insecurity. They are the least likely to believe in the American dream. Jim Edwards (2015) characterizes the generation as more conservative, more money-oriented, and more pragmatic about money. It has been suggested by Turner (2015) that the 9/11 attacks and the recession of 2008 have left this group unsettled and insecure. Benhamou (2015) states that this generation wants everything, everywhere, and now, and are always in a rush and somewhat impatient. He describes this group as stressed out by their way of perceiving the world—a bleak future, especially in regard to the economy and environment. However, they do want to succeed, achieve, and contribute to a better world, and they are very inclined in community volunteerism. Levit (2015) states they don't just want a job—they want fulfillment and excitement from their employment that helps in moving our world forward.

Spirituality was more predominant in past generations, and in part this made it very acceptable for one's own life to be structured. For instance, our values called for getting a high school education or higher, obtaining employment, getting married, having children, purchasing a home, and supporting the family. Today, the poor status of the Western economy, demographics, and a shortsighted elite have contributed to restraining the upward social mobility of the young. The generation is therefore financially handicapped and has learned the hard way not to want or to live like previous generations. This is why young adults grow up with no real path in life. I may be overgeneralizing, but the aspiration in life for many in Generations X and Y is to go to school in order to develop a career that pays well in order to buy many things, rather than a more traditional approach to their lives in which marriage and family is the driving force. After all, who can afford the lifestyle of recent past generations anyway? An unstable employment scene and poor financial outlook translates into people wanting less and leading simpler lives. The American or Canadian dream is accessible to fewer folks. Our young have less to look forward to. Yet because capitalism only financially rewards those who go with the system, our young are brainwashed to believe that if one works extremely hard, they will be rewarded. Perhaps at one time this was the case, especially when Western economies were based on the expanding primary and secondary sectors. But in the vast tertiary sector that has developed, hard work does not necessarily translate into financial security. In fact, we work harder today than ever before, and our incomes don't show it. During the 1990s, salaries decreased, and in 2016 the cost of living continues to rise, but our salaries do not keep pace. We are feeling the effects of higher taxation.

I believe it is more important to teach that reward for hard work is not solely tied to money. Reward and satisfaction can also be attained in many other ways, including sitting down with each other and communicating sincerely in the best interests of the parties concerned. This is virtually nonexistent today. We are so busy making money that we don't even have time to process what someone else is trying to convey to us, and we miss the meaning of what is said; this includes the manner in which we communicate with our young. What about collaboration? What about doing something for someone else? No way—time is money! We are so focused on money that we judge people by how much wealth they have accumulated.

Perspective and priority are the keywords we must remind ourselves of, because someone out there is trying to blur these two factors for their own reasons and benefit. The reason is that they want your money. They spend millions on advertising and go to extremes to influence your emotions in order to convince you to buy goods and services and a lifestyle they are offering. They don't care about your health or your environment, they don't care about your credit card debts, they don't care about you or your family, and they don't care about your future! They simply want your money. They want you to aspire to have it all. Of course, I am referring to the corporation. I say you should aspire less, and then you will appreciate more and keep your life in perspective and balance. If one aspires for all, life becomes a struggle. Is there a need for this? The beauty of the capitalist system is that you have the right to choose. The trends and subtle changes in Western thought tend to lean toward a shifting away from capitalist thinking. It's kind of relieving to think that capitalism as we know it will one day be part of history. Prepare for a shift in thought.

The Environment: Values and Economics

While I am on the topic of economics, I want to elaborate on the economic costs associated with environmental degradation. The costs will be quick, direct, and harsh should we not curb environmental problems. You see, one environmental issue is linked to another and another, and eventually that link is with the economy and then us, because it is the natural world that sustains our anthropogenic activities. Break just one link in the realm of the natural world, and ripple effects are felt in a dependent industry and then by the public. Let me elaborate further.

Imagine the negative economic impacts associated with decreasing ozone levels in the atmosphere. Tourism, the biggest industry in the world, would be hard hit because many would shy away from destinations and activities having to do with the sun. Imagine the setback felt with associated forward and backward linkages in the tourism economy. Let's say the famous tourist destination of Jamaica becomes known as a destination where ozone levels are known to be dangerous to one's health. Tourists would stop going there. Airliners would lose revenues from that line of air traffic, and a decrease in air travel could cause the airline to lay off employees because of losses and profit margins. In Jamaica, hotels and their staff, boutiques and their staff, restaurants and their staff, craftsmen, entertainers, and farmers would feel the economic and financial repercussions of decreased travel to their island. Why? It would happen because one important link in the economic system was damaged, the ozone layer, which is part of the complex environmental system.

Let's use another example: the economic implications involved with global warming. It is predicted that a two- to three-degree Celsius increase in global temperature could arise because of anthropogenic activities, particularly of the last 130 years or so of industrialization. The impact of this change in temperature has an economic cost in terms of how it affects many industries, the backbone of our industrialized society. It also affects our values. By this I refer to the fact that in Canada, a warmer climate would mean the elimination of the ski season, affecting the entire economy of that industry. But it would create better agriculture because the growing season would be longer. Thus, the ski resorts would suffer, and the farmers would gain. It therefore also becomes a question of values, because what is good for some is not good for others when the environment forces us to alter our ways of doing things. On a wider scale, our entire world economy would be changed. The question becomes, could humanity react quickly enough to such dramatic shifts in the environment and still be economically healthy? If we are to keep things as they are, are we willing to give up the convenience of the automobile, a cost in terms of values or activities that contribute to global warming? I hope I have demonstrated the strong link between the environmental system and economic system, and the costs associated with both in terms of dollars and morals, values, and beliefs.

Speak and Be Heard

In my opinion, the bulk of Western society does not speak its mind on issues that concern them every day, because we live in a system that listens only to those who have accumulated great wealth or power. Many feel it is not their place to speak out because they are not considered important due to lack of money and clout. This is wrongful thinking because one does not have to be rich or powerful to be heard. One must surpass the fear of being humiliated by others. One requires the strength to withstand the criticism from those who are ignorant of the ills of capitalism or have their own interests to protect. Imagine how many social issues would not have been given attention or evolved without the student movement, the feminist movement, the black rights movement, the environmentalist movement, the antiwar movement, and the like, particularly in the United States during the 1960s. The people involved with such organizations went through great pain to be heard. I am not necessarily in support of all the tactics that were used during that era to get their message across, but it is a reminder of how important it is to express our points of view, even if they appear to not support capitalism. After all, it's not just about the buck, it's about how we live our everyday lives as human beings. Your right is to express yourself by voting for candidates that represent your opinions at the federal, provincial, and municipal levels of government. You feel good about the fact that you did the right thing and exercised your right to vote. Is that enough? Does that vote really change how you live or how the environment is protected? We must express our points of view diplomatically; sometimes merely casting a vote is not good enough.

Those who are docile in nature, convey a pleasant demeanor, and want good are often perceived as naive or weak, or they are belittled. However, they are probably well-rounded and secure people. I can think of American President Jimmy Carter as a leader who was often wrongly judged during his tenure. In my mind, Jimmy Carter is one of the best presidents America ever had. Docile people don't feel the need to speak aggressively or be aggressive; they are strong enough inside to make up their own minds on things and not necessarily go with the flow. They are full of what I call quiet determinism. They contribute to society in their own way, and they should never be discounted or labeled. In my view, these are also people who can bring about change for the better, and they are the ones who give with their hearts, seek meaningful relationships, and would rather negotiate in the best interests of both parties.

Everyone is important for this world. Do not reject but beware of those who have not yet understood what it means to be in harmony with the world. Stay strong in front of those who think they know everything there is to know about you and who only see and hear what they select to fit their own biased perception. These are not the times for individualism or big actions with no meaning; these are times that require love and care, spirituality, sincerity, empathy, honesty, forgiveness, respect, humbleness, meaningful communication, sense of community, and consciousness of the natural world. It is important not to frown upon, discriminate against, or belittle anyone. By treating people as people, it brings out the best in all of us. Ask yourself, have we been treating blacks fairly? Have we been treating natives fairly? Have we been treating third world people fairly? Perhaps if we realize that we are all in this world for one purpose, to do good, we would treat each other in better ways. All these virtues can come from the family, an institution that is not supported culturally as it should be. All these virtues must be exported outside the boundaries of the family, imported into our wider society, and remembered even in the most trying of times.

A New System

What have we become? The current employment market treats individuals as commodities, as if those who are more marketable advance and others don't, even though they may have the drive and potential to do well. This is capitalism at its finest because the law of supply and demand is applied to people. The problem is that society itself has let this happen.

It has even reached a point where industry controls your mind because it tells you what you want, and then you demand it. Are you that foolish? Is industry giving you what you want, or is industry teaching you how to want and need their product? You're the only one who can stop industry from telling you what you want, need, and cherish. We have adopted a lifestyle that is dictated to us. Are you tired of being told what to do by government, the company you may be working for, the industries, and selective societal conformity? I predict another way of living for all will come, where the goal is physical health, serenity, spirituality, and harmony between individuals and cultures and the natural world. People will eventually come to the realization that our current way to live has been forced upon us by those who stand to make a profit. We don't have to abide. This transition will have to be made with great care, discipline, and peace, and it should be in the best interests of all, including the natural world. We can start anew during peacetime, just as we did after both World Wars. We need a focal and independent body to guide and ease the process. I am not referring to the abrupt dismantlement of capitalism in its current form, but the evolution of a system that is more gentle and caring. In its place, we could adopt the system I call ecohumanism. Yes, the ecohumanist or ecohumanistic system and society!

Alas, my worry is not with words to name the new system. No matter its name, my concern is with inherent human weaknesses (such as greed, jealousy, ignorance, lack of understanding, the need for power, physical strength, and age) as determinants of leadership in social organizations. These are some of the worrisome traits that would be transferred to the new ecohumanist system, and that would limit its potential. It is these traits that we need to improve because these are the same traits that made the capitalist system evolve, mature, damage, and in many instances destroy. You can call me a dreamer if you want, but this is the way we must think if we want a better world, because capitalism goes against this sort of reasoning and new vision for the world. Nobody ever said we must go the capitalist way; we can proceed in a new direction. After all, as someone once said, spaceship earth did not come with a how-to manual.

Time for Common Sense

What can I say? Wealthy or poor, during the post–World War II period, most of us were brought up in a manner that was full of love, security, good mannerisms, and spirituality. We were encouraged to do good and be good individuals, and to view life and all people as good. Was this the dream the parents of the post-war era wanted for their children? They were on the right track in these regards. What happened? Did too much affluence spoil the dream for subsequent generations, letting us forget the simpler things in life? Simple, caring, and courteous gestures and words helped us live together. These days, we search for happiness and meaning in our lives. Are these virtues related to how much we carry in our pockets, or are they supposed to be part of us having more or less money? I know a lot of people who were not very wealthy, but they were very happy. Are the new generations trying to provide themselves the secure and healthy middle- to upper-middle-class lifestyle they were shown by their parents, but they can't obtain it today because of economic restraints over which they have no control? Is this the root of our societal frustrations? Tell me, who is right or wrong these days? Consensus on many important issues isn't there. Everyone's opinion and way to live seems to be correct, and everybody has his own profound reasons for taking the stand he does. But are we getting anywhere politically, economically, socially, culturally, and environmentally?

I would have to say the word that describes Western society the best today is confusion. I believe the second word that characterizes today is insecurity. In my mind, I think the 1950s to the 1990s are the decades that opened up a new can of worms. Until the questions surrounding this period are dealt with and answered, there will not be communal peace of mind. The way the issues can be resolved in the next decades of the new millennium is to think simply and develop our emotional and spiritual health! Avoid threatening distractions, get down to the basics, and adopt a nurturing attitude toward life and people, rather than a competitive and individualistic one. The lack of this simplicity in today's Western society and our individual lives is what is making our lives harder today. I hope that in the next decades, the goal will be to regain social perspective, composure, and posture.

Just a few decades ago, there used to be more social order, and gender roles were more clearly defined. The nuclear family unit worked well, and emotional needs were satisfied. Today, I like the fact that Western women are independent and no longer subservient to males, but I can't help but wonder whether or not familial lifestyles were better in the recent past. Woman have made their point, and rightfully so, that they can excel in all areas of work and life in general, and this is now widely acknowledged and accepted. But, for the sake of a better familial and societal quality of life, isn't it better for one of the partners in a marriage or relationship not to work, especially during child-rearing years? Already there exists evidence that suggests large numbers of women would be willing to stay at home and bring up their children if they could afford it. Wouldn't one partner not working full time make family life better and more pleasant? It becomes a question of what we want. Do we want to run around like chickens without heads in order to maintain a highly materialistic lifestyle, or would we rather settle for less material wealth and stress, and more familial love, security, calmness, and quality time? Is simple common sense calling out to us to adopt certain positive societal attributes of the recent past?

The Western laissez-faire nature of this day and age is good for nobody, including the natural world, and three-quarters of the world population that still lives in third world conditions. Let's share rather than sink; let's be more ecohumanistic.

Conclusions

So, where do we stand? We have investigated why and how Western thinking has changed over the last five hundred years, and how it has spatially diffused geographically and shaped the world we live in today. It can be called the new Western colonization of the world. Western civilization's quest for capitalistic economic expansion, where cities offer the strategic settings for these intentions, stems from reductionist-mechanistic attitudes that were implanted in the sixteenth and seventeenth centuries. Linear, reductionist thinking has led to Western domination particularly through the use of manly, aggressive intentions and technology in pursuit of ultimate capitalistic economic growth and political power. In order to attain and maintain higher economic prosperity from one generation to the next, the Western world has never hesitated in absorbing areas of the now underdeveloped world and the circumpolar north into its sphere of influence and control. By the same token, the West has inadequately considered the negative impacts of her actions on the social, cultural, economic, political, and environmental fabrics of different global societies she has encountered during her quest. Even though significant parts of the world have benefited little from Western dominance, the West herself currently faces many social, economic, and environmental challenges unseen before stemming from her own path toward "development," and the West is now facing a major transformation with the simultaneous slow decline of the patriarchal system, the fossil fuel age, and cultural shifts in values and beliefs.

Generally, the Western way of thinking, including mass consumerism and the associated heavy reliance on technology, causes an illusion of continued prosperity and advancement. It is more clear now than ever that our way of thinking in purposeful, involuntary, or inadvertent ways takes humanity ten steps backward for every one step of progress. This is confirmed when one considers environmental problems caused by anthropogenic activity, such as inadvertent global climatic change, soil erosion, deforestation, acid rain, endangered wildlife and plant life, nuclear and domestic and industrial terrestrial waste disposal, ozone depletion, pollution, pressures on nonrenewable resources, worldwide exponential population growth, issues such as misdistribution of wealth, world hunger, and social and familial dysfunction. Nonetheless, our politicians still favor economic growth. Western governments have been good in promoting growth through the use of geopolitics because they justify their reasons for war, conflict resolution, freedom, and democracy for their nations in nationalistic mannerisms, "in the best interest of the nation."

It is well-known that Western foreign policy and intervention is often purely for creating political and economic stability, which is essential for driving the Western capitalist economy. With regard to the environment, corporations have always responded to the political need for more economic growth by steadily increasing production and consumption over the past 130 years, causing many environmental problems. Technologies and environmental management systems designed to eliminate or reduce the by-product from the manufacturing process and eventual consumer disposal of goods have not kept up. Added to this is the fact that environmental protection does not generate a profit for manufacturers and is a frowned-upon expense for governments. The corporate world and governments refuse to acknowledge the economic implications of a degraded environment because acknowledgment of long-term perils will require a shifting of financial attention to areas of activity that will upset the agenda of capitalist thinking and programming. Neglected environmental problems will eventually come to a point that merit vast financial attention from both private and public budgets; the issue of global climatic change is a leading example of this. Already we are witnessing the fear of a slowing of the economies of the Western world from business lobbyists in view of government efforts at resolving or diminishing environmental problems. Governments are often forced to sidestep targets established to lessen various environmental problems in view of economic considerations such as economic recovery from recessions or industry interest groups.

There exists a light at the end of the tunnel, however. What is referred to as a subculture comprehends the disastrous ways of Western thinking. The subculture consists of the women's movement, environmentally concerned groups and citizens, movements focusing on better social conditions, antiwar movements, spiritual movements, the antinuclear movement, and now the scientific community; these groups are challenging the old value system and view of the world. In this light, the subculture is the driving force behind change for the better. Science will continue to influence Western society because this community now acknowledges that the universe is not a machine and that scientific thinking does not necessarily have to be reductionist and mechanistic; holistic and ecological views are also scientifically sound. It is this subculture that will propel humankind into the coming solar age, and it will plant the seeds of the new human condition founded on new thinking, values, and beliefs that will harmonize with Mother Earth and her peoples. Leading nations must realize in due time that change must come quickly enough and be flexible enough to accommodate a new world view that will allow humankind to proceed toward and reach the solar age with a sane society and a nurturing planet, because until now, humanity's contemporary experience on earth has been one of soap opera proportions in which the characters are faced with one problem after another.

The urbanized Western world must realize that what is experienced by each human on a day-to-day basis is human-made, quasisuperficial, and not natural. It is things such as man-made concrete, paved roads, traffic congestion, traffic lights, superstructures; worries about money and power, greed, ignorance, jealousy; conformity, stereotyping, labeling, prejudging, discrimination, misunderstandings, and lack of fair and meaningful communication between peoples. The existence of social stratums, the social demands put on women and men because of gender, crime, world poverty and child labor; polluted air, noise emanating from machines, competition, economic uncertainties, employment insecurity, limitations of time, work hours established by humans; and human perfectionism as defined by the mass media and the movie industry all contribute, in a mixed and confusing manner to superficiality around us and imbed in our minds and collective thoughts on a daily basis, therefore causing imbalances in our individual lives. These imbalances are threatening our individual power, freedom, creativity, sense of fulfillment, personal satisfaction, personal sense of security, peace of mind, and mental and physical health. It is in fact these same imbalances that lead us to collectively hurt the environment and each other.

Perhaps it is time we realize that we must integrate our souls more with nature, a sense of spirituality, empathy toward others and living things, a heightened respect for individual rights, self-respect and dignity, and a lifestyle that is more in tune with the natural human pace. Because of routine daily imbalance in our individual lives caused by many factors such as those mentioned above, it is small wonder that we look at the world around us with an inward perspective that results in virtual, inadvertent, individual selfishness in which one looks after himself more than his neighbor, community, nation, hemisphere, or globe. Bertalanffy advocated that we dare to broaden our perspective from nation to globe, and maybe we may have to broaden our perspective from individual to globe! Perhaps if humanity proceeds at a more human pace—a pace not dictated by government and the needs and desires created by corporate advertising, the economy, technology, or a work environment—individuals can have more freedom to absorb what is really around them, including people and nature. This may heighten their appreciation of themselves, other people, and nature. Perhaps then we can allocate time and concern for the health of our planet and the status of the human condition, and we can give renewed importance to the universal institution of the nuclear family as the basic foundation of a proper society.

There are too many distractions around us taking our priorities away from our individual well-being and our families. There are certainly too many messages out there, especially of individualism and personal freedom, that affect the psychology of individuals and couples, often leading to separation, divorce, and the demise of the nuclear family unit. On a bigger scale, these distractions don't allow our society to properly focus on wider issues such as those related to the natural environment and what is taking place in poorer parts of the world and the circumpolar north.

As Westerners—and, I include other populations around the world because of the globalization of Western thinking—we have become less spiritual and religious, less empathetic toward others and the natural world and more distanced from nature, more mechanical in the Newtonian-Cartesian sense, harder, less tolerant, and less patient. We are less community oriented, more money oriented and business-minded, more technological and materialistic, more self-sustaining and self-fulfilled, less concerned for others, less family oriented, and more alone. Too many of our decisions regarding life come down to "What's in it for me? Does it make financial sense?" This is called bottom-line thinking. The factors sustaining capitalism force us to think in this manner, or else the majority can't survive within it. Many of our individual behaviors, beliefs, or actions such as assertiveness, aggressiveness, and competition must be in line with capitalist thinking in order for us to succeed, and this takes us away from a more wholesome self and better relationships with others. By extension, you may not be at issue because the capitalist economy forces one to abide by certain rules, behaviors, protocols, standards, and approaches, allowing you to make something of yourself and support yourself and your family.

Succeeding in our economic system means one is actually contributing to it and perpetuating it.

Our political leaders and corporate elite are grappling with keeping afloat our current economic system and way of life. There is still hope when considering the many people (including participative private enterprise) who give their time to community service and financial contributions to social and environmental causes. There are amazing organizations such as CARE, Doctors without Borders, CUSO International, UNICEF, the David Suzuki Foundation, Greenpeace, Habitat for Humanity, the Clinton Foundation, the Lions, and Optimist International. They demonstrate that there is still something innate within us that desires good, and this is a huge part of the foundation required on the road to a more evolved, composed, postured, and nurturing Western and world society.

If the reader recalls, in the introduction of this work, it was Anthony explaining to cousin Sam what the documentary on television was all about. Toward the conclusion of his description, Anthony's brother accidentally bumps into him, and he happens to spill some wine on the sofa. Anthony therefore stops talking momentarily to clean the sofa. When the conversation resumes, Sam asks Anthony, "How does the documentary end?"

Anthony replies, "I don't know. It's 'to be continued.'"

Bibliography

Aboriginal Healing Foundation. "Suicide among Aboriginal People in Canada." Ottawa, Ontario, Canada, 2007 (retrieved online April 25, 2016).

Abu-Lughod, J., and Richard Hay Jr., eds. *Third World Urbanization*. Toronto: Routledge Library Editions, 2007.

Albrecht, E. C. "Alcohol Abuse in Alaska." *Polar Record* 21, no. 135 (September 1983): 601–602.

Alexander, C. *Angry Society*. Saskatoon: Yellowknife Publishing Company Ltd., 1976.

Anderson, M. A. "Comparison of Anthropometric Measures of Nutritional Status in Preschool Children in Five Developing Countries." *American Journal of Clinical Nutrition* 32 (November 1979): 2339–2345.

Armstrong, E. *The Circumpolar North*. London: Methuen, 1978.

Armstrong, Warwick. "Access to Food: An Approach, An Overview." Montreal, Québec: Centre for Developing Area Studies, McGill University, Paper No. 1 (April 1985).

Arroyo, G. "Institutional Constraints to Policies for Achieving Increased Food Production in Selected Countries." *The World Food Conference of 1976.* Des Moines: Iowa State University Press, 1977.

Bajpai, Prableen. "The World's Top 10 Economies." *Investopedia.* June 24, 2016 (retrieved online June 25, 2016; www.investopedia.com).

Balandier, Georges. *Political Anthropology.* Baltimore: Penguin Books, 1972.

Bassi, Daniele. "From Child Hunger to Obesity: Brazil's New Health Scourge." *The Guardian,* May 19, 2014 (retrieved online April 25, 2016).

Benhamou, Laurence. "Everything You Need to Know about Generation Z." *Business Insider,* February 12, 2015 (retrieved online April 27, 2016).

Brody, H. "Industrial Impact in the Canadian North." *Polar Record* 18, no. 115 (1977): 333–339.

Buchanan, Anne. *Food, Poverty, and Power.* Nottingham, England: Spokesman Books, 1982.

Burrascano, Giovanni. *The Great Chain of Being and Our Vainglorious Western Civilization: A Brief Understanding of the Great Chain of Being and the Interconnected Forces Affecting Western Thinking and the World Over the Last Five Hundred Years.* Self-published, 2002. Found in the National Library of Canada, Ottawa, Ontario.

Canadian Press. "Ontario Health Minister Announces $2 Million in Aid for Attawapiskat." *The Globe and Mail*, April 13, 2016 (retrieved online April 27, 2016).

Capra, Fritjof. *The Turning Point*. New York: Bantam Books, 1983.

Hanks, Christopher C., Gary Granzberg, and Jack Steinbring. "Social Changes and the Mass Media: The Oxford House Cree, 1909–83." *Polar Record* 21, no. 134 (1983): 459–465.

Costa, R. M. B. Levantamento do Estado Nutricional de Criancas em Idade Preescolar. Porto Alegre: Servico de Nutricao Escolar, 1970.

Davidson, Mark. "General Systems Theory: A Prescription for Survival." *Uncommon Sense: The Life and Thought of Ludwig Bertalanffy, Father of General Systems Theory*. Boston: J. P. Torcher Inc., 1983.

Davis, Kingsley. "The Urbanization of the Human Population." *Scientific American* 213, no. 3 (1965): 40–53.

deBlij, H. J. *Human Geography—Culture, Society, and Space*. New York: John Wiley & Sons, 1977.

Dorea, J. G. *"Nutritional Status and Zinc Nutriture in infants and Children in a Poor Urban Community of Brazil." Journal of Ecology of Food and Nutrition* 12 (1982): 1–6.

Dos Santos, Theotonio. "The Structure of Dependence." *American Economic Review* 60 (May 1970): 231–236.

Edwards, Jim. "Goldman Sachs Has Made a Chart of the Generations … And It Will Make the Millennials Shudder." *Business Insider UK*, December 5, 2015 (retrieved online June 25, 2016).

Edwards, Lin. "Humans Will Be Extinct in 100 Years Says Eminent Scientist." PhysOrg.com, June 23, 2010 (retrieved online May 2, 2016).

Eveleth, P. B., and J. M. Tanner. *World-Wide Variations in Human Growth*. Cambridge: Cambridge University Press, 1976.

Frank, André Gunder. "The Development of Underdevelopment." *Latin America: Underdevelopment or Revolution*. New York: Modern Reader Monthly Review Press, 1969.

Feder, Ernest. "The Peasants' Perspectives in Underdeveloped Countries." *Monthly Review; An Independent Socialist Magazine*. Volume 27, Number 1, New York, May 1975: 14–28. Published by The Monthly Review Foundation.

Financial Post. "Greenhouse Deal to Bring 'Hardship.'" October 10, 1997, p. 4.

Frank N. Magid & Associates. "The First Generation of the Twenty-First Century." April 30, 2012, http://magid.com/sites/default/files/pdf/MagidPluralistGenerationWhitepaper (retrieved online April 27, 2016).

Friedl, J. "Lactase Deficiency: Distribution, Associated Problems, and Implications for

Nutritional Policy." *Journal of Ecology of Food and Nutrition* 11 (1981): 37–48.

George, Susan. *How the Other Half Dies: The Real Reasons for World Hunger.* Harmondsworth; New York: Penguin, 1976.

Gomez, Eduardo. "Tackling Brazil's Obesity Problem. *"Americas Quarterly: Politics, Business and Culture in Our Hemisphere,* June 27, 2012 (retrieved online June 25, 2016).

Graham, G. G. "Nutritive Value of Brown and Black Beans for Infants and Small Children." *American Journal of Clinical Nutrition* 32 (November 1979): 2362–2366.

Hamelin, L. E. *Canadian Nordicity: It's Your North, Too.* Montreal: Harvest House Ltd., 1979.

Haraldson, S. A. S. "Health and Disease Among Lapps." *Polar Record* 21, no. 133 (1983): 345–357.

Holmes, R., J. Hagen-Zanker, and M. Vandemoortele. "Brazil's Story: Social Protection in Brazil: Impacts on Poverty, Inequality and Growth." Overseas Development Institute, London, 2011 (retrieved online April 27, 2016).

Honigmann, J. J. *"Adaptations in Canadian Circumpolar Towns" Consequences of Economic Change in Circumpolar Regions,* L. Muller-Wille, J. P. Pelto, R. Darnell, eds. Edmonton, Alberta, Canada: Boreal Institute for Northern Studies, the University of Alberta, 1975, p. 149–162.

Hustich, I. "The Population of the Arctic, Subarctic, and Boreal Regions." In *Polar Geography* 3, no. 1 (1979): 40–48.

Keith, R. F., and B. J. Wright. *Northern Transitions, Vol. II.* Ottawa: Canadian Arctic Resource Committee, 1978.

Khazan, Olga. "Why Brazil Loves Breastfeeding." *The Atlantic,* December 14, 2015 (retrieved online April 30, 2016).

Knight, P. T. "Health, Nutrition, and Education." *Brazil Human Resources Special Report.* Washington, DC: The International Bank for Reconstruction and Development, 1979, annex III, p. 1–113.

Latin American Regional Reports. LARR-RB-84-05, June 1, 1984, p. 3.

———. LARR-RB-84-06, July 6, 1984, p. 3.

———. LARR-RB-85-02, February 1985, p. 2.

Leineweber, Markus. "Modernization and Mental Health: Suicide among the Inuit in Greenland." PhD dissertation, Department of Cultural Psychology, University of Nijmegen (the Netherlands), March 10, 2000 (retrieved online April 27, 2016).

Levit, Alexandra. "Make Way for Generation Z." *The New York Times.* March 28, 2015 (retrieved online June 25, 2016).

Lovejoy, Arthur. *The Great Chain of Being.* Harvard University Press, 1998.

Meadows, Donella H., Dennis L. Meadows, Jørgen Randers, and William W. Behrens, III.

The Limits to Growth. New York: Signet Books, 1975.

Mitchell, B., and D. R. W. Sewell. *Canadian Resource Policies: Problems and Prospects.* Toronto: Methuen, 1981.

Monteiro, Carlos Augusto. "The Decline of Child Malnutrition in Brazil." Facultade de Saude Publica, Universidade de Sao Paulo, Sao Paulo, Brasil, 2009 (retrieved online April 25, 2016).

Muller-Wille, L. "Snowmobiles among Lapps." *NORD-NYTT,* no. 4 (1971).

Muller-Wille, L. "Population Concentration in Arctic and Subarctic Ethnic Groups." *Consequences of Economic Change in Circumpolar Regions.* L. Muller-Wille, J. P. Pelto, R. Darnell, eds. Edmonton, Alberta, Canada: Boreal Institute for Northern Studies, the University of Alberta, 1975, p. 123–136.

Muller-Wille, L., and J. P. Pelto. "Introduction." *Consequences of Economic Change in Circumpolar Regions.* L. Muller-Wille, J. P. Pelto, R. Darnell, eds. Edmonton, Alberta, Canada: Boreal Institute of Alberta, 1975, p. 1–11.

Mumford, Lewis. *The Transformations of Man,* New York: Harper, 1956.

Mumford, Lewis. "Closing Statement," *The Ecological Conscience.* Disch, Robert, ed. New York: Prentice-Hall, 1970.

Nebel, Bernard J. *Environmental Science: The Way the World Works.* Englewood Cliffs, New Jersey: Prentice-Hall Inc., 1981.

Nooter, G. "Changes in Social Habits Caused by New Elements in Material Culture." *Consequences of Economic Change in Circumpolar Regions* L. Muller-Wille, J. P. Pelto, R. Darnell, eds. Edmonton, Alberta, Canada: Boreal Institute for Northern Studies, the University of Alberta, 1975, p. 37–47.

North, Douglas C. *The Economic Growth of the United States 1790–1860.* Englewood Cliffs, New Jersey: Prentice-Hall, 1961.

Olson, Robert. "Canada's Aboriginal Communities and Suicide: Called to Listen, Called to Understand." *InfoExchange* 11 (2013): 1–5 (retrieved online: May 5, 2016).

Pelto, J. P. "Ecology, De-Localization and Social Change." *Consequences of Economic Change in Circumpolar Regions.* L. Muller-Wille, J. P. Pelto, and R. Darnell, eds. Edmonton, Alberta, Canada: Boreal Institute for Northern Studies, the University of Alberta, 1975, p. 29–36.

Reid, Angus. *Shakedown: How the New Economy Is Changing Our Lives.* Seal Books, McClelland-Bantam Inc., 1997.

Roberts, Bryan. *Cities of Peasants.* London: Edward Arnold Ltd., 1981.

Rohmer, R. *The Arctic Imperative.* Toronto: McClelland and Stewart Ltd., 1973.

Sater, J. E., ed. *The Arctic Basin.* Washington, DC: The Arctic Institute of North America, 1969.

Sen, Amartya. *Poverty and Famines: An Essay on Entitlement and Deprivation.* Oxford University Press, 1983.

Schumacher, E. F. *Small Is Beautiful: A Study of Economics as if People Mattered.* London: Sphere Books Ltd., 1974.

Sindell, P. S. "Some Discontinuities in the Enculturation of Mistassini Cree Children." *CHANCE.* Conflict in Culture: Problems of Developmental Change Project. Ottawa: Canadian Research Center for Anthropology, Université Saint-Paul, 1968.

Sjoberg, Gideon. "The Origin and Evolution of Cities." *Scientific American* 213, no. 3 (1965): 54–63.

Smith, D. "The Mackenzie Delta Domestic Economy of the Native Peoples." Mackenzie Delta Research Project, Rep. No. 3. Ottawa: Northern Coordination and Research Center, Dept. of Indian Affairs and Northern Development.

Stirling, I., and W. Calvert. "Environmental Threats to Marine Mammals in the Canadian Arctic." *Polar Record* 21, no. 134 (1983): 433–449.

The World Bank *Table: Mortality Rate Under-5 (per 1,000).* The World Bank Group, 2016 (retrieved online June 25, 2016; data .worldbank.org).

Turner, Anthony. "Generation Z: Technology and Social Interest." *Journal of Individual Psychology* 71, no. 2 (2015): 103–113 (retrieved online November 19, 2015).

Waltz, J. "Civilization, Good and Bad, Invades the Canadian North." *PolarTimes* 72 (1972): 8–9.

Wolf, Eric R. *Europe and the People without History.* Los Angeles: University of California Press Ltd., 1982.

Wonders, W. C. *Canada's Changing North.* Toronto: McClelland and Stewart Ltd., 1971.

Wonders, W. C. "Northern Resource Development." *Canadian Resource Policies: Problems and Prospects.* S. Mitchell and D. Sewell, eds. Toronto: Methuen, 1981, p. 56–83.

Wright, Harrison. *The "New Imperialism" Analysis of Late-Nineteenth-Century Expansion.* Lexington, Massachusetts: D. C. Heath and Company, 1976.